Innovative Learning Analytics for Evaluating Instruction

Innovative Learning Analytics for Evaluating Instruction covers the application of a forward-thinking research methodology that uses big data to evaluate the effectiveness of online instruction. Analysis of Patterns in Time (APT) is a practical analytic approach that finds meaningful patterns in massive data sets, capturing temporal maps of students' learning journeys by combining qualitative and quantitative methods. Offering conceptual and research overviews, design principles, historical examples, and more, this book demonstrates how APT can yield strong, easily generalizable empirical evidence through big data; help students succeed in their learning journeys; and document the extraordinary effectiveness of First Principles of Instruction. It is an ideal resource for faculty and professionals in instructional design, learning engineering, online learning, program evaluation, and research methods.

Theodore W. Frick is Professor Emeritus in the Department of Instructional Systems Technology in the School of Education at Indiana University Bloomington, USA.

Rodney D. Myers is Instructional Consultant in the School of Education at Indiana University Bloomington, USA.

Cesur Dagli is Research Analyst in the Office of Analytics & Institutional Effectiveness at Virginia Polytechnic Institute and State University, USA.

Andrew F. Barrett is Co-founder of ScaleLearning, Inc. and leads the Learning Technology team at Shopify, Inc., Canada.

Innovative Learning Analytics for Evaluating Instruction
A Big Data Roadmap to Effective Online Learning

Theodore W. Frick, Rodney D. Myers, Cesur Dagli and Andrew F. Barrett

NEW YORK AND LONDON

First published 2022
by Routledge
605 Third Avenue, New York, NY 10158

and by Routledge
2 Park Square, Milton Park, Abingdon, Oxon, OX14 4RN

Routledge is an imprint of the Taylor & Francis Group, an informa business

© 2022 Theodore W. Frick, Rodney D. Myers, Cesur Dagli and Andrew F. Barrett

The right of Theodore W. Frick, Rodney D. Myers, Cesur Dagli and Andrew F. Barrett to be identified as authors of this work has been asserted by them in accordance with sections 77 and 78 of the Copyright, Designs and Patents Act 1988.

All rights reserved. No part of this book may be reprinted or reproduced or utilised in any form or by any electronic, mechanical, or other means, now known or hereafter invented, including photocopying and recording, or in any information storage or retrieval system, without permission in writing from the publishers.

Trademark notice: Product or corporate names may be trademarks or registered trademarks, and are used only for identification and explanation without intent to infringe.

Library of Congress Cataloging-in-Publication Data

A catalog record for this title has been requested

ISBN: 978-1-032-00018-3 (hbk)
ISBN: 978-1-032-07735-2 (pbk)
ISBN: 978-1-003-17634-3 (ebk)

DOI: 10.4324/9781003176343

Typeset in Times New Roman
by Apex CoVantage, LLC

Contents

Foreword ix
Preface xi
Chapter Summaries xvii
List of Tables, Figures, and Maps xx

1 **Learning Journeys in Education** 1
  Metaphor of a Journey: The Oregon Trail 1
  The State-Trait Approach to Measurement: Quantitative Methods 2
  Individual Episodic Stories: Qualitative Methods 3
  Qualitative Temporal Mapping that is Quantifiable and Generalizable: A Third Alternative for Educational Research Methods 4
  The Larger Problem in Educational Research 5
  References 6

2 **Overview of the Big Study** 9
  A Tale of Two Learning Journeys 9
    Learning Journey #1: Sam's Case 9
    Learning Journey #2: Melinda's Case 13
  Design and Structure of IPTAT Using First Principles of Instruction 18
    Problem-Centered Principle 18
    Activation Principle 18
    Demonstration Principle 19
    Application Principle 19
    Integration Principle 19

Results from 936,417 Learning Journeys through IPTAT in the Big Study in 2019 and 2020 20
    Activation Results 22
    Demonstration Results 23
    Application Principle 24
    Integration Principle 25
    Overall Unique Pageviews 25
What Does All This Mean? 25
References 27

3 The Indiana University Plagiarism Tutorials and Tests   28
Introduction 28
Major Redesign of IPTAT in 2015 30
    Authentic Problems Principle 31
    Activation Principle 31
    Demonstration Principle 34
    Application Principle 34
    Integration Principle 35
    Certification Tests 35
    Summary of Changes to the Newly Designed IPTAT in 2015 38
        What's the Same? 39
Usage of IPTAT from 2019 and 2020 40
    Minimalists 41
    Traditionalists 42
    Dabblers 42
    Registrants 42
    User-Developer Feedback Loop 43
What About COVID? 44
References 45

4 More Details of the Big Study   46
Discovery of Google Analytics for Doing APT 46
Important Concepts for Doing Analysis of Patterns in Time 48
    Two Fundamental Ways of Temporal Segmenting: Prediction and Retrodiction 48
    Temporal Segmenting by Quarters One at a Time 49
    Retrodictive APT Queries 50
        Endpoint Condition Defined 50
        Users Who Passed 50

    Users Who Have Not Passed 50
    Apply the Endpoint Condition to the GA Audience
      Reporting Tool (UA) 50
    Using GA to Find Matches of Pageviews within
      Segments 51
    Wash, Rinse, and Repeat, then Combine 53
    Some Key Issues We Identified and Resolved to do APT of
      IPTAT Data Streams Created by GA 53
    Can You Do APT with GA4? 56
    Who Are the Registered IPTAT Users in 2019 and 2020
      (from Our MySQL Database at IU)? 59
    Summary 62
    References 62

5 Analysis of Patterns in Time as a Research Methodology   63
    Introduction 63
    APT of Direct Instruction and Academic Learning Time:
      Joint Event Occurrences 64
      Linear Models Approach 65
      APT Approach 65
    APT of Teacher-Student Interaction in Class: Frequency
      of Sequential Events 66
    APT of Asynchronous Online Discussion: Sequential
      Patterns of Comments 68
    APT Outside of Education 72
      Moneyball 72
      Google Analytics 74
    References 75

**6 Using Analysis of Patterns in Time for Formative
    Evaluation of a Learning Design**   78
    Introduction 78
    Simulation Fidelity 79
    Evaluation of Fidelity 80
    Using APT for Model Verification 81
    The Diffusion Simulation Game 82
    Applying the APT Procedure to the DSG 83
    Data Analysis and Results 86
    Conclusion 89
    References 90

7 Analysis of Patterns in Time with Teaching and Learning Quality Surveys 93

APT of Course Evaluations 93
The Goal: Creating a Table from a Spreadsheet 94
Formation of TALQ Scales 95
Transferring MOO-TALQ Survey Responses to a Spreadsheet 97
Creating Spreadsheet Formulas for Each TALQ Scale 98
Creating Further Derived Scores for Scale Agreement (Yes or No) 99
Creating a Table for the Combinations of Categories 100
Summary 102
References 103

8 Analysis of Patterns in Time as an Alternative to Traditional Approaches 104

Making Inductive Inferences with APT 104
Big Data in Education 107
Approaches to Big Data 108
Methods Used to Analyze Big Data 108
Learning Analytics and Instructional Design 109
The Value of Theory to Guide Educational Research 110
Extending APT 112
References 112

Epilogue 115
Abbreviations and Symbols 125
Index 129

Foreword

Innovative Learning Analytics for Evaluating Instruction:
A Big Data Roadmap to Effective Online Learning

It is very gratifying when an instructional designer uses *First Principles of Instruction* to guide the development of a course. However, it is almost unbelievable and more than a bit overwhelming when that course reaches more than 700,000 learners. I'm very grateful that Dr. Frick and his associates decided to revise their very popular and important online plagiarism course using First Principles of Instruction. It is even more gratifying to learn that when these students study the parts of the course based on First Principles, they are approximately four times more likely to pass the Certification Test.

Analysis of Patterns in Time (APT) is a very innovative approach to the evaluation of students' learning journeys. This book makes an important contribution by describing and illustrating this methodology. APT implemented via Google Analytics provides a very important tool for evaluating massive amounts of learning data as illustrated by the "Big Study" described in this book.

While Dr. Frick and I had visited about my work earlier, it wasn't until he and his colleagues applied APT to student evaluations of their courses that I became aware of this approach to learner evaluation. The Teaching and Learning Quality (TALQ) scales provided one of the first validations of my claim that learning effectiveness is correlated with the degree to which First Principles of Instruction are implemented. When students self-reported that the instruction they experienced in a course involved problem-solving, demonstration, and application, their performance in the course, as judged both by themselves and their instructors, was better than the performance of students in similar courses who did not indicate that they had experienced instruction based on these principles.

The Big Study reported in this book compared the learning paths of students who were able to pass the Certification Test with those who were not. Most students were able to eventually pass the Certification even when they failed on earlier tries, but only after pursuing a path through the learning materials that were based on First Principles of Instruction. While this study does not provide a direct comparison of instruction based on these principles with instruction not based on these principles, it nevertheless demonstrates that engaging in instruction based on First Principles makes it far more likely that a student will pass the test.

This book is a very good manual for using APT as an important tool for evaluating instruction. As MOOCs, massive open online courses, become more popular and as any individual course reaches many more students than in the past, this book will assist you to be able to use this powerful tool to evaluate these courses. APT is a very important contribution to the future of learning analytics.

M. David Merrill

Preface

The Big Picture

If you were an investor, and you could choose between a company that is not likely to use effective business strategies and a company that is three to five times more likely to use them, where would you put your money? Likewise, if you could use methods of education that were three to five times more likely to help students succeed in their learning, would you?

Drawing on decades of experience as a teacher, instructional designer, and education researcher, Merrill (2002) proposed five principles common to a variety of instructional design theories, principles that he believes lead to effective, efficient, and engaging learning. Merrill named these the First Principles of Instruction (FPI) and hypothesized that instruction that fails to implement one or more of these principles will result in a "decrement in learning and performance" (Merrill, 2013, p. 21). He went on to write "the support for this hypothesis can only come from evaluation studies for a given instructional product or research comparing the use and misuse of these principles" (Merrill, 2013, p. 21).

In this book, we describe our efforts to apply FPI in the redesign of an online learning resource, the Indiana University Plagiarism Tutorials and Tests (IPTAT), and how we empirically evaluated the effectiveness of FPI using Analysis of Patterns in Time (APT), a powerful method for finding meaningful patterns in massive datasets. We document the extraordinary effectiveness of FPI for promoting online learning. In brief, we found that students who passed an IPTAT Certification Test were three to four times more likely per learning journey to choose instructional activities designed with FPI, when compared with unsuccessful students. These findings were based on over 936,000 learning journeys by students located in 213 countries and territories worldwide, mostly between the ages of 14 and 44. These findings are based on big data collected over two years, 2019–2020.

We provide a roadmap for educators and researchers to follow for both online and in-person instruction, and we illustrate through concrete examples how to document instructional effectiveness with Analysis of Patterns in Time. For those who teach students in-person, we provide a practical alternative for measuring effectiveness. We illustrate how we used student perceptions of Teaching and Learning Quality (TALQ) when coupled with instructor assessments of student mastery of course objectives. We used APT here as well and what we found for face-to-face courses was similar. Students who agreed that they experienced FPI and successful engagement were between three and five times more likely to be independently rated by their instructors as high masters of course objectives.

What this Book is About

Our main goal in this book is to show how APT can be used as a practical and powerful way to evaluate the effectiveness of online instruction. What is new in this book is the application of APT as an innovative way to do learning analytics of big data on online teaching and learning.

APT is a proven methodology that differs from traditional qualitative and quantitative approaches to measurement (Frick, 1983, 1990; Frick & Dagli, 2016; Myers & Frick, 2015). APT is a way to analyze *student learning journeys*. Student learning journeys are a new way to capture temporal maps of what students do. In APT, patterns of learning are themselves *qualitative*, whereas counting occurrences of those patterns within learning journeys is *quantitative*.

We show through specific examples how we have used APT to answer the question: how well do First Principles of Instruction promote student learning? We primarily use the Indiana University Plagiarism Tutorials and Tests (IPTAT) as the recurring example. You can view IPTAT at: https://plagiarism.iu.edu. We encourage you to try IPTAT yourself, as you read parts of this book.

IPTAT is a type of a MOOC: a massive open online course. IPTAT is relatively short in duration, taking about two hours to complete. Numerous instructors in colleges, universities, and secondary schools typically utilize IPTAT as an assignment for their students to complete on their own outside of class meetings. Students typically choose parts of IPTAT to help them pass a Certification Test. Instructors want their students to learn to recognize plagiarism, so they will not commit plagiarism in the future.

What is also innovative in this book is that we show how Google Analytics can be used to do APT. Google Analytics is a free service that that can be incorporated into your website in order to track how users interact with it pageview by pageview. Google Analytics allows you to create reports on usage of a website by applying a variation of APT methodology. You can also use Google Analytics to observe in real-time the number of current users of your website, what they are viewing, and where they are located.

We hope that this book provides a roadmap for how you and others can evaluate effectiveness of online instruction and learning. When you are finished with this book, you should have learned enough so that when you design your own instructional website, you will have at your fingertips an easy-to-understand but powerful way to determine its effectiveness. You should also be able to investigate the effectiveness of *different* design principles and instructional strategies—by following the same approach as we have illustrated in this book for First Principles of Instruction.

If you are interested in evaluating the effectiveness of in-person instruction in traditional learning settings, where teachers and students meet face-to-face in classrooms, we provide an alternative way you can use APT. We illustrate past research with the Teaching and Learning Quality (TALQ) Scales. TALQ Scales can be used to obtain student perceptions of the quality of their instruction and learning at or near the end of a course or training workshop. When student responses to questions on the TALQ instrument are aggregated, we illustrate how teaching effectiveness can be determined through APT methods. This approach is an alternative to building websites and tracking student usage as we have done with IPTAT. Using TALQ requires no technical knowledge of website development and can be done using a paper-and-pencil format for collecting student evaluations.

If more of us do this kind of disciplined inquiry, then, over time we will collectively advance knowledge of effective educational practices. As educators subsequently adopt these more effective practices, students will be more likely to succeed in their learning endeavors. We will improve education. More effective education should improve the quality of life for everyone.

What You Need to Know before You Start

There are many resources for learning how to make web pages and websites, including dynamic websites that require scripting in programming languages such as PHP or Python. There are numerous resources on how to store computer data collected via the Web, such as using database systems and query languages such as MySQL. You should use these resources if need be, since our book will not address these kinds of know-how, though we do occasionally refer to some of these elements. Most likely you will need to form a design team with members who have these different kinds of skills, much as we have for IPTAT. And have everyone on your team read this book, of course!

You and your team members do not need a degree in statistics or research methodology to understand our major approach to analysis of big data: *Analysis of Patterns in Time* (APT). Since APT is not currently taught in typical research courses and is not discussed in other books at this time, this book will help you understand APT and how you can use it. You do not need a Ph.D. to understand APT, or any degree at all. If you can count, add, subtract, multiply, and divide numbers, if you understand percentages and how to form proportions, and if you can compute simple averages (arithmetic means), then you should be able to understand APT. In its most basic form, APT is no more complicated than computing a baseball player's batting average by counting the number of times at bat and how many times that player got a base hit. For example, if a player went to bat 100 times and got 40 base hits, then they have a batting average of 0.400 (40 divided by 100). This means that 40 percent of the time when *that batter* faced a pitcher in a baseball game, they made a base hit.

Or suppose you and your friend went on a diet to lose weight. You each weigh yourself once a week on your scales over a period of 52 weeks, so you can determine how many pounds per week you lost. You each just add up the pounds you lost that year, and then divide the result by 52 weeks in order to determine how many *pounds per week* you lost. Suppose that you lost two pounds per week, and your friend lost one-half pound per week. You could claim that you lost four times as much weight per week as did your friend (by dividing 2 by 0.5). Or you could count kilograms and make a similar comparison, as long as you are counting the same units for both of you (or other measures such as inches or centimeters of reduced waist size).

You also need a sense of time when observing one event that follows another. For example, if you observe that clouds in the sky normally form *before* it rains or snows, then you are noting a temporal sequence of events. But it does not rain or snow every time clouds form, just some of the time. For example, it might be the case that, in your location, when clouds are present, then it rains or snows 15 percent of the time. You could also say that when clouds are overhead, the likelihood of rain or snow is 0.15 in your location. You might also observe that it *never snows* when clouds are present *and* the outside air temperature is above 40 degrees Fahrenheit (or 4 degrees Celsius). In its most basic form, APT is no more complicated than this: what are the chances that an event occurs when certain conditions are true? In our book, we want to determine that when students pass a test, what conditions are true when compared with students who have not passed a test?

Finally, if you can use a calculator, such as an app on your smartphone or computer, then you can more quickly carry out the arithmetic required for APT. And you'll need a computer with an Internet connection that runs a web browser such as Firefox, Chrome, Safari, Edge, or Opera. We assume that you already know how to browse the Web and can use a web browser.

For Whom is this Book Intended?

Our main target audiences are those who do:

- Instructional design and development,
- Online and in-person instruction, or
- Educational research and evaluation.

We further anticipate a worldwide target audience. Effectiveness of online and in-person learning is relevant to education everywhere, not just limited to the U.S. Due to the novel coronavirus pandemic, many schools and universities have been recently offering more online and hybrid instruction.

We believe that this book will be further useful in many other disciplines where effective means to achieve ends are valued.

Ways to Read this Book

If you are a teacher or instructional designer, Chapters 1, 2, 3, and 7 should be of most interest. These four chapters introduce the concept of learning journeys, the main findings of our Big Study, how we designed our online instruction with First Principles, and how we have previously evaluated in-person instruction using the Teaching and Learning Quality scales.

If you do educational research and evaluation, you should read the whole book. The first chapter and the last five chapters emphasize the major differences between Analysis of Patterns in Time (APT) and traditional quantitative and qualitative research methods. In the last half of the book, we provide further examples of how APT was used in other research studies, in addition to the Big Study described in the first four chapters.

We have kept this book as short as possible, in order to help readers quickly grasp the main ideas—trying to balance breadth and depth. In addition to bibliographic references, we provide hyperlinks to supplementary information that is particularly relevant and which should be available on the Web for years to come. If you are reading the digital version, you can just click on or tap the links as needed, and then return to the book to continue. Since it is the publisher's policy to direct *external* hyperlinks to respective main pages for those websites, and not to specific pages within websites, you may to need copy and paste (or type) the entire URL into your Web browser to see the exact webpage.

We have avoided specific step-by-step directions about how to use software tools such as Google Analytics and Microsoft Excel because they are likely to change over time, and because we ourselves have adapted to changing digital technologies over the past six decades. Instead, we describe our overall strategies and how we adapted those tools to do Analysis of Patterns in Time. Nonetheless, you should be able to follow the examples in order to replicate what we did. When APT was invented and conceived in the 1970s, there were no microcomputers or smartphones, and there was no World Wide Web. When we started this book, we were using Google's Universal Analytics (UA). By October 2020 Google had supplemented UA with Google Analytics 4, which we discuss and further illustrate near the end of Chapter 4.

Finally, we provide brief summaries at the beginnings of each chapter to highlight the main points. We further provide transitional information and cross-referencing in many places for those who read chapters out of order. With decades of web design experience among the authors, this book is designed as a hybrid of both print and digital resources that can be accessed in a variety of ways. We provide a number of different routes in our roadmap for your own learning journeys.

References

Frick, T. W. (1983). *Nonmetric temporal path analysis: An alternative to the linear models approach for verification of stochastic educational relations* [Unpublished doctoral dissertation]. Indiana University Graduate School.

Frick, T. W. (1990). Analysis of patterns in time (APT): A method of recording and quantifying temporal relations in education. *American Educational Research Journal, 27*(1), 180–204.

Frick, T. W., & Dagli, C. (2016). MOOCs for research: The case of the Indiana University plagiarism tutorials and tests. *Technology, Knowledge and Learning, 21*(2), 255–276.

Merrill, M. D. (2002). First principles of instruction. *Educational Technology Research & Development, 50*(3), 43–59.

Merrill, M. D. (2013). *First principles of instruction: Identifying and designing effective, efficient, and engaging instruction*. Pfeiffer.

Myers, R., & Frick, T. W. (2015). Using pattern matching to assess gameplay. In C. S. Loh, Y. Sheng, & D. Ifenthaler (Eds.), *Serious games analytics: Methodologies for performance measurement, assessment, and improvement* (Chapter 19, pp. 435–458). Springer.

Chapter Summaries

Chapter 1: Learning Journeys in Education

Chapter 1 introduces the concept of a *learning journey*. We use the Oregon Trail as a metaphor to explain why traditional quantitative and qualitative research methods are inadequate for capturing learning journeys. On the other hand, temporal maps do capture learning journeys, and Analysis of Patterns in Time (APT) can be used to count occurrences of qualitative patterns in temporal maps. We discuss the fundamental limitations of traditional qualitative and quantitative research approaches for determining effectiveness of instructional methods.

Chapter 2: Overview of the Big Study

In Chapter 2 we apply APT to a large-scale study of the effectiveness of First Principles of Instruction within the online Indiana University Plagiarism Tutorials and Tests (IPTAT). We begin by illustrating two typical cases of learning journeys: Sam and Melinda. We next summarize the results from our Big Study of over 936,000 learning journeys during 2019 and 2020. We demonstrate how we found that, on average in each learning journey, successful students were nearly four times more likely to utilize unique parts of IPTAT which were designed with First Principles of Instruction, when compared with unsuccessful students.

Chapter 3: The Indiana University Plagiarism Tutorials and Tests: 2002 through 2020

Chapter 3 describes how we redesigned the IPTAT in 2015 using First Principles of Instruction (FPI). We provide examples of IPTAT web pages and learning activities that illustrate FPI: sequencing tasks from simple to complex; activation of prior knowledge; demonstration of skills to be learned; application of newly acquired skills to solve problems; and integration of new skills in one's everyday life. We also describe how we created trillions of Certification Tests to measure student success in classifying word-for-word, paraphrasing, and non-plagiarism when viewing original source materials and samples of student writing. We conclude by describing two years of IPTAT usage, where there were nearly 36.5 million pageviews. We note three general kinds of usage patterns: minimalists, traditionalists, and dabblers.

Chapter 4: More Details of the Big Study

In Chapter 4 we report on our Big Study in greater detail, which was previewed in the second chapter. We demonstrate how we arrived at our findings over a two-year interval, by illustrating APT for one quarter, and then we describe how we combined quarters using a spreadsheet. The Big Study involved students from 213 countries and territories worldwide, mostly between 14 and 44 years old. We describe how Google Analytics was used to track IPTAT usage. Then we illustrate how segmenting of temporal maps and logical conditions were applied via Google Analytics in order to carry out parts of APT queries. We further illustrate how we used a spreadsheet with cell formulas to complete the APT calculations. We provide further details on how Google Analytics identifies users. We conclude by summarizing demographic characteristics of students who registered to take IPTAT Certification Tests.

Chapter 5: Analysis of Patterns in Time as a Research Methodology

Chapter 5 discusses APT in greater detail. We provide several historical examples of use of APT as a research method. We then describe use of APT concepts outside of educational research. One example is *Moneyball*, which is the story of how the Oakland Athletics professional baseball team used sabermetrics in evaluating players. This helped the Oakland A's field winning teams at a fraction of the cost of player salaries paid by other successful Major League Baseball teams. The second example is Google Analytics, which provides a web tracking service to help their business clients determine advertising strategies and patterns of usage that lead to increased sales of the clients' products and services.

Chapter 6: Using Analysis of Patterns in Time for Formative Evaluation of a Learning Design

Chapter 6 provides a further example of how APT has been used for improving an online simulation game. We used APT to improve the fidelity of the online Diffusion Simulation Game (DSG) by evaluating the congruence of DSG gameplay processes and outcomes with empirical research on adoption of innovations. We illustrate how APT was used to identify several inconsistencies of DSG gameplay outcomes with outcomes expected from theory and empirical research on diffusion of innovations. This then allowed us to correct several mistakes in DSG algorithms and then to further use APT to verify that the changed algorithms did indeed improve DSG fidelity. The DSG has been played hundreds of thousands of times by more than 18,000 registrants from 2014 through 2020.

Chapter 7: Analysis of Patterns in Time with Teaching and Learning Quality Surveys

Chapter 7 describes an alternative way to determine instructional effectiveness that can be used in a wide range of learning environments—for both online and in-person instruction. The alternative is to have students complete an evaluation instrument called the Teaching and Learning Quality (TALQ) Scales. Students rate their instruction and learning experiences without knowing what First Principles of Instruction are. They rate their experiences by responding to a random mix of Likert-type items. They also rate their own academic learning time (ALT, which is successful engagement), learning progress, satisfaction with the course and instructor, and overall quality of their experience. We provide examples from several studies of how TALQ was used with APT methods to determine effectiveness of FPI and ALT. The advantage of TALQ is that if it is used appropriately, teachers and researchers can determine instructional effectiveness without the technical knowledge and skills required for building websites such as IPTAT.

Chapter 8: Analysis of Patterns in Time as an Alternative to Traditional Approaches

Chapter 8 reviews the change in perspective which we have provided in this book. When we focus on temporal patterns, we can predict what leads to successful learning outcomes. By making inductive inferences from APT results, predictable patterns of instructional effectiveness can be identified. We further contrast APT with other existing approaches to learning analytics. We conclude by discussing the value of theory for APT and its further extension to MAPSAT: Map and Analyze Patterns and Structures Across Time.

Epilogue: The 50-Year Journey to Writing this Book

The Epilogue tells the story of the serendipitous discovery of Google Analytics as a way to do Analysis of Patterns in Time. It concludes by describing the 50-year journey that has culminated in this book. Acknowledgments follow.

Tables, Figures, and Maps

Tables

2.1	IPTAT Big Study: Structure of Tutorials and Tests Designed with First Principles of Instruction	21
2.2	Google Analytics Data on IPTAT Usage: Big Study 2019–2020	22
2.3	Temporal Patterns per Learning Journey (n = 936,417 Journeys): Big Study 2019–2020	24
4.1	Basic IPTAT Audience Usage Statistics for 2020 Quarter 1: Jan. 1–Mar. 31	52
4.2	Unique Views of IPTAT Web Pages Designed with First Principles of Instruction for 2020 Quarter 1: Jan. 1–Mar. 31	52
4.3	Derived Measures from Table 4.1 for 2020 Quarter 1	52
4.4	Mean Unique Views of IPTAT Web Pages per Learning Journey that Were Designed with First Principles of Instruction for 2020 Quarter 1	53
4.5	APT via GA4 Segmenting: First Principles of Instruction Goals Achieved in IPTAT between December 20, 2020 and January 18, 2021	58
5.1	Temporal Relationships of Teacher Instruction and Student Engagement	66
6.1	Projected Distribution of Games by Number of Adoption Points Obtained	87
6.2	First Dataset: Distribution of Games by Number of Adoption Points	87
6.3	First Dataset: Frequency and Scores of Activities for 100 Games	88
6.4	Comparison of Descriptive Statistics for Games	89
6.5	Third Dataset: Distribution of Games by Number of Adoption Points	89

Tables, Figures, and Maps xxi

7.1	Data from Frick, Chadha, Watson, and Zlatkovska (2010b) Study Used to Do Analysis of Patterns in Time	94
7.2	Construction of MOO-TALQ Scales	98
7.3	Results for the APT Query for Each First Principle for the GR Group	99
7.4	Results for the APT Query for Each First Principle for the UG Group	99
7.5	Results for the APT Query for GR Students: If Agree that FPI and ALT Occurred, then Student Mastery is ___?	101
7.6	Results for the APT Query for UG Students: If Agree that FPI and ALT Occurred, then Student Mastery is ___?	101

Figures

2.1	IPTAT Welcome Page	10
2.2	Mean Unique Pageviews for Certificants and Non-Certificants in the Big Study	23
3.1	Home Page of the Original Tutorial, circa 2003	29
3.2	Annual Pageviews of the Indiana University Plagiarism Tutorial and Tests (IPTAT), from 2003 through 2020.	30
3.3	Screenshot of IPTAT "Welcome" Page in 2020	32
3.4	Five Levels of Difficulty in Recognizing Plagiarism	33
3.5	Example of the Activation Principle for Advanced Level of Problem Difficulty	33
3.6	One of 12 Screencasts that Illustrate Plagiarism and How to Fix It, for the Demonstration Principle	34
3.7	Example of the Application Principle at the Advanced Level of Problem Difficulty	35
3.8	Example of Feedback to an Incorrect Answer for the Application Principle at the Advanced Level of Difficulty	36
3.9	Example of a Reflection Activity, for the Integration Principle at the Advanced Level of Problem Difficulty	37
3.10	Example of the IPTAT Certification Test Starting Page	37
3.11	Example of Certification Test Feedback when Passing	38
3.12	Example of Certification Test Feedback when Not Passing	39
3.13	Example of a Primary Level Certificate when Passing	40
3.14	Daily IPTAT Pageviews from Google Analytics between January 1, 2019 and December 31, 2020 (total of 36,485,235 pageviews)	41
4.1	Reported Age of Registrants in Years: IPTAT 2019–2020	59
4.2	Highest Level of Education Achieved: IPTAT 2019–2020	60
4.3	Why Are You Considering This Tutorial? IPTAT 2019–2020	61

| 4.4 | Current Levels of Understanding Plagiarism: IPTAT 2019–2020 | 61 |
| 5.1 | The Linear Models Approach to Analyzing a Relation. Regression Equation: $EN = 0.40DI + 0.57$. $R^2 = 0.33$. | 64 |

Maps

2.1	Temporal Map for IPTAT User Sam	11
2.2	Temporal Map of Session 1 for IPTAT User Melinda	13
2.3	Temporal Map of Session 2 for User Melinda	15
5.1	Coding Example Adapted from Joyce Koh's Dissertation (2008, p. 38)	67
5.2	Simplified Excel Spreadsheet to Illustrate Feedback Pattern Identification and Counting	70
6.1	Temporal Map of the First 12 Turns in a Game	84

1 Learning Journeys in Education

Summary: We introduce the concept of a *learning journey*. We use the Oregon Trail as a metaphor to explain why traditional quantitative and qualitative research methods are inadequate for capturing learning journeys. On the other hand, temporal maps do capture learning journeys, and Analysis of Patterns in Time (APT) can be used to count occurrences of qualitative patterns in temporal maps. We discuss the fundamental limitations of traditional qualitative and quantitative research approaches for determining effectiveness of instructional methods.

Metaphor of a Journey: The Oregon Trail

Education is a temporal process. Teaching and learning occur through intervals of time. Education is analogous to a journey, such as following the Oregon Trail. The destination we often want to reach in education is successful student learning achievement. Teachers provide the guidance to help students reach the destination. From a practical perspective, we want to document what makes some trips more successful than others. If other educators who come along later follow routes that have previously been successful, then *their* students would be expected to benefit also.

The Oregon Trail was a major route that early U.S. settlers traveled in the mid-1800s from what is now Independence, Missouri, near Kansas City, to the Columbia River Valley, near what is now Portland, Oregon (see https://en.wikipedia.org/wiki/Oregon_Trail). Lewis and Clark were pioneers who successfully made the trip in the early 1800s largely by horseback, canoes and rafts, and on foot, mostly by following the Missouri and Columbia Rivers with help from native Americans along the route. Later, settlers traveled by covered wagons pulled by oxen, on horseback, with many walking. The winding 2,200-mile trip took many months and was perilous. Some travelers died on the trip; and others never made it to Oregon, settling in places along the route. Those who did make it often arrived with very little food and belongings. Many travelers lost weight or died due to malnutrition and disease during the trip. Diseases took more lives than anything else, including cholera, dysentery, typhoid fever, and diphtheria. In that sense, those who were fortunate succeeded, but survivors often were somewhat poorer and weighed less when they arrived at their destination.

Fast-forward to May 2020.

Many people now can get to Portland from Kansas City by driving an automobile and by taking interstate highways. According to Google Maps, the trip should take about 27 hours of driving time. If stopping overnight to rest, then the trip might take three driving days, travelling about 600 miles each day. A minivan could be rented to transport five passengers and their luggage for about $500, plus the additional cost of fuel, two motel rooms for two nights of lodging, food purchased for meals along the way, etc. A conservative estimate of the cost of the 1,800-mile trip would be approximately $300 per person, assuming expenses and motel rooms are shared.

Another way to make that trip is to fly on commercial passenger airlines. For example, Southwest Airlines offers one-way fares for about $400 for an adult that will typically take seven to ten hours, depending on stops and plane changes. Two bags, 50 pounds or less, can be taken as luggage with no extra charge.

Finally, for the more wealthy, private jets can be chartered. A web search in May 2020, indicated that the one of the least expensive flights would cost approximately $18,000 for three hours of flight time in a small jet for six passengers, or approximately $3,000 per person. Flights can often be scheduled to depart and arrive when convenient for passengers. These jets typically have more comfortable seating and more amenities.

The State-Trait Approach to Measurement: Quantitative Methods

In this approach to research, we measure states or properties of individual persons, things and conditions at various points in time. Using quantitative research methods, we might conduct an Oregon Trail Study by assessing personal wealth, a person's weight at the start and end of the trip, duration of the trip, and overall cost. In effect, the above description characterized states and traits of those individuals at various points in time for different classes of people and different eras. Separate measures would be taken: cost per person in U.S. dollars, weights of each person and their luggage, trip duration in hours, whether or not the destination was reached, and the personal wealth of each individual when the trip begins and ends.

A quantitative study using a linear models approach (LMA) would most likely find an inverse linear relationship between cost of trip and its duration. Trips that take less time cost more. For wealthy individuals, a charter jet rental would not appreciably change their personal wealth. For someone with only $1,000 in personal savings, a charter flight would leave them several thousand dollars in debt. For most individuals in 2020, their weight would not appreciably change when measured at the start and end of the trip, while that would not be true for many early settlers in the 1800s, who arrived at their destination emaciated and starving.

Suppose we did take independent measures such as these on a sample of 500 individuals who took trips from Kansas City to Portland, Oregon in the mid-1800s and early 2020.

Here is what we would likely find. Richer people complete the trip in less time than poorer travelers. There would be a negative linear relationship between personal wealth and trip duration. Greater wealth would be associated with shorter trips. If we look at the relationship between individuals' weight lost during the trips, early settlers would have lost more weight on average, whereas travelers in 2020 would not appreciably change their weight. Overall, there would be a positive linear relationship. Trips of longer duration would be associated with more weight lost. More deaths also occurred during the longer trips, also a positive linear relationship—statistically speaking.

Without information about what happened *during* the trip, it would be difficult to explain the weight loss. Moreover, why is it that richer people make the trip in less time? Without additional information about modes of travel, speed along the way, routes taken, relative costs, and causes of deaths and not finishing the trip (i.e., dropouts), it would be unclear why.

For educational research using quantitative methods, this approach is descriptive of thousands of studies from the 1960s to the present. Quantitative research studies typically use a state-trait method of measurement, and statistical linear models are used to relate those measures (Kirk, 1999, 2013; Tabachnick & Fidell, 2018). In effect, snapshots are taken at each point in time, but there is often lack of information about what happened between the snapshots.

Individual Episodic Stories: Qualitative Methods

When using qualitative research methods that are narratives, we essentially tell episodic stories (e.g., Creswell & Creswell, 2018; Creswell & Poth, 2018). For example, consider the trip made by Lewis and Clark in the early 1800s. Then compare it with a trip taken by Bill Gates in 2020, who is a multi-billionaire and could easily afford his own private jet. Telling unique stories about their contrasting trips might be quite interesting and illuminating, but it would be unwise to make any generalizations about all Oregon Trail travelers from this non-random sample of two trips.

4 *Learning Journeys in Education*

In qualitative research, we may discover some interesting common patterns in the unique stories, but generalizability of findings is on shaky grounds. For example, Lewis, Clark, and Gates became famous men, who were willing to take risks when younger. Samples are typically very small. Sampling error and lack of generalizability to larger populations is a paramount criticism. Rich, detailed descriptions of a few cases may provide insight into what is happening in education, but it makes it difficult to generalize about what educational methods are more effective than others. It makes it difficult to predict educational outcomes in general—about what is likely to make a difference in *successful* learning.

Qualitative Temporal Mapping that is Quantifiable and Generalizable: A Third Alternative for Educational Research Methods

There is another way to approach this, referred to as Analysis of Patterns in Time (APT). The state-trait approach does not capture event-by-event temporal details, even so-called time-series analysis methods. The state-trait approach is analogous to taking still photographs. What happens *between* those snapshots is often unknown. As a further example, use of box scores to characterize baseball games exemplifies the state-trait approach.

On the other hand, APT temporal maps are analogous to "documentary movies" about what happens at various times to students and teachers *during* their educational journeys. APT temporal maps can describe learning journeys as well as other temporal processes. Temporal maps consist of coded episodic events, as are coded stories in qualitative methods. A temporal map of a baseball game describes what happened *during* the game, not just the total runs scored and which team won.

However, unlike qualitative methods, APT *queries* can subsequently identify *patterns of events within* temporal maps. This can help identify activities that are more or less successful in helping students reach their learning destinations. When temporal maps are representative of large populations, results of APT queries are generalizable to those populations (Frick, 1990). Analyzing temporal maps of professional baseball games can help identify patterns and strategies that lead to a team's winning season, year in and year out.

APT has been around for several decades, and the benefits of such an approach have been demonstrated in a number of educational research studies (An, 2003; Barrett, 2015; Dagli, 2017; Frick, 1983, 1990, 1992; Frick et al., 2008; 2009; 2010; Howard et al., 2010; Koh, 2008; Koh & Frick, 2009; Lara, 2013; Luk, 1994; Myers, 2012; Myers & Frick, 2015; Plew, 1989; Yin, 1998). A major obstacle to adoption by educational researchers has been the time and effort required to create temporal maps, as well as lack of adequate software for subsequently querying collections of such maps (see https://aptfrick.sitehost.iu.edu/).

It's relatively easier to measure a few things independently and apply linear models, or to observe a few cases and write detailed descriptions. Nonetheless, APT techniques have been used *outside* of education with well-documented success (e.g., *Moneyball*; Lewis, 2004), especially now with big data and large arrays of computers doing parallel processing. Perhaps the most successful application of APT is *Google Analytics* (2005: https://en.wikipedia.org/wiki/Google_Analytics, https://analytics.google.com/analytics/academy/course/6). It is further likely that APT is used in *proprietary* extant artificial intelligence systems which use pattern matching for making predictions (see Segaran, 2008; Segaran & Hammerbacher, 2009).

With increasing use of the World Wide Web by billions of people, websites which are used for research purposes can now provide rich data sets that consist of temporal maps. Google has been doing this tracking since 2005. Google Analytics is the current hardware/software platform that allows vast amounts of temporal data to be collected through large computer data centers which utilize state-of-the art parallel processing systems (so-called "cloud computing", e.g., https://en.wikipedia.org/wiki/Cloud_computing; https://computing.llnl.gov/tutorials/parallel_comp/). While Google typically sells these services to business clients whose goal is to make a profit, these Google services can also be used by educational researchers who know how to leverage them, even for free.

While APT can be done locally on laptop computers and tablets, or basically on any computing devices including smartphones, this is on a very miniscule scale when compared to Google cloud computing. The real computing power is in the cloud, and computers we touch with our hands are the clients, such as running web browsers, which access the cloud computers via the Internet.

The Larger Problem in Educational Research

It is therefore not surprising that educational research has largely failed to provide widely *generalizable* empirical results supporting educational methods that are more effective than others. Since the Coleman et al. (1966) study we have known, for example, that there is a positive relationship between socioeconomic status (SES) and student learning achievement as measured by standardized tests. Little else makes a significant difference in learning achievement after statistically controlling for SES, which accounts for a large proportion of the variance in student achievement, when taking a state-trait approach to measurement and using linear models for investigating relationships among variables. Linear models include multiple and logistical regression, factor analysis, canonical analysis, path analysis, discriminant analysis, ANOVA, MANOVA, ANCOVA, hierarchical linear models, time-series analysis, and the like (Kirk, 1999, 2013; Tabachnick & Fidell, 2018). When using traditional quantitative research methods, we measure things *separately*, and then we try to verify relationships among those measures.

What we need is strong, empirical, and generalizable evidence to document methods of education that are more effective than others, widely accessible to educators, more cost-effective, and more efficient (Fischer et al., 2020). To do this, we also need research *methods* that can document what happens during such educational journeys.

APT is clearly one such method. We illustrate the power and practicality of APT by example in this book. Perhaps, as did Lewis and Clark for the Oregon Trail, we will establish a trail for other researchers to follow in the future who are attempting to add to praxiological knowledge of education.

Next, in Chapter 2 we present an overview of what we call the Big Study. We illustrate by example a way to address limitations of traditional qualitative and quantitative research methods. In this Big Study we demonstrate the creation of temporal maps for tracking student interaction with the online Indiana University Plagiarism Tutorials and Tests (IPTAT). We then illustrate how we used APT to analyze learning journeys characterized by those maps. We show how we segmented nearly 1.87 million temporal maps (i.e., big data) in order to evaluate the effectiveness of First Principles of Instruction (Merrill, 2020).

References

An, J. (2003). *Understanding mode errors in modern human-computer interfaces: Toward the design of usable software* [Unpublished doctoral dissertation]. Indiana University Graduate School.

Barrett, A. F. (2015). *Facilitating variable-length computerized classification testing via automatic racing calibration heuristics* [Unpublished doctoral dissertation]. Indiana University Graduate School.

Coleman, J. S., Campbell, E. Q., Hobson, C. J., McPartland, J., Mood, A. M., Weinfeld, F. D., & York, R. L. (1966). *Equality of educational opportunity*. Washington, DC: U.S. Government Printing Office. http://www.google.com/books/edition/Equality_of_Educational_Opportunity/TdRf6VHr2RgC?hl=en&gbpv=1&printsec=frontcover

Creswell, J. W., & Creswell, J. D. (2018). *Research design: Qualitative, quantitative and mixed methods approaches* (5th ed.). SAGE.

Creswell, J. W., & Poth, C. N. (2018). *Qualitative inquiry and research design: Choosing among five approaches* (4th ed.). SAGE.

Dagli, C. (2017). *Relationships of first principles of instruction and student mastery: A MOOC on how to recognize plagiarism* [Unpublished doctoral dissertation]. Indiana University Graduate School.

Fischer, C., Pardos, Z., Baker, R. S., Williams, J. J., Smith, P., Yu, R. . . . Warschauer, M. (2020). Mining big data in education: Affordances and challenges. *Review of Research in Education, 44*, 130–160.

Frick, T. W. (1983). *Nonmetric temporal path analysis: An alternative to the linear models approach for verification of stochastic educational relations* [Unpublished doctoral dissertation]. Indiana University Graduate School.

Frick, T. W. (1990). Analysis of patterns in time (APT): A method of recording and quantifying temporal relations in education. *American Educational Research Journal, 27*(1), 180–204.

Frick, T. W. (1992). Computerized adaptive mastery tests as expert systems. *Journal of Educational Computing Research, 8*(2), 187–213.

Frick, T. W., Chadha, R., Watson, C., Wang, Y., & Green, P. (2009). College student perceptions of teaching and learning quality. *Educational Technology Research and Development, 57*(5), 705–720.

Frick, T. W., Chadha, R., Watson, C., & Zlatkovska, E. (2010). Improving course evaluations to improve instruction and complex learning in higher education. *Educational Technology Research and Development, 58*(2), 115–136.

Frick, T. W., Myers, R., Thompson, K. R., & York, S. (2008). *New ways to measure systemic change: Map & Analyze Patterns & Structures Across Time (MAPSAT).* Featured research paper presented at the annual conference of the Association for Educational Communications & Technology, Orlando, FL.

Google Analytics. (2005–present). Retrieved July 6, 2020, from https://en.wikipedia.org/wiki/Google_Analytics

Kirk, R. E. (1999). *Statistics: An introduction* (4th ed.). Harcourt Brace.

Kirk, R. E. (2013). *Experimental design: Procedures for the behavioral sciences* (4th ed.). SAGE.

Koh, J. H. (2008). *The use of scaffolding in introductory technology skills instruction for pre-service teachers* [Unpublished doctoral dissertation]. Indiana University Graduate School.

Koh, J. H., & Frick, T. W. (2009). Instructor and student classroom interactions during technology skills instruction for facilitating preservice teachers' computer self-efficacy. *Journal of Educational Computing Research, 40*(2), 207–224.

Lara, M. (2013). *Personality traits and performance in online game-based learning: Collaborative vs. individual settings* [Unpublished doctoral dissertation]. Indiana University Graduate School.

Luk, H.-K. (1994). *A comparison of an expert systems approach to computer adaptive testing and the three-parameter item response theory model* [Unpublished doctoral dissertation]. Indiana University Graduate School.

Merrill, M. D. (2020). *M. David Merrill's first principles of instruction.* Association for Educational Communications and Technology.

Myers, R. D. (2012). *Analyzing interaction patterns to verify a simulation/game model* (Order No. 3544908) [Doctoral dissertation]. Indiana University. ProQuest Dissertations and Theses Global.

Myers, R. D., & Frick, T. W. (2015). Using pattern matching to assess gameplay. In C. S. Loh, Y. Sheng, & D. Ifenthaler (Eds.), *Serious games analytics:*

Methodologies for performance measurement, assessment, and improvement (Chapter 19, pp. 435–458). Springer.

Plew, T. (1989). *An empirical investigation of major adaptive testing methodologies and an expert systems approach* [Unpublished doctoral dissertation]. Indiana University Graduate School.

Segaran, T. (2008). *Programming collective intelligence: Building smart Web 2.0 applications*. O'Reilly.

Segaran, T., & Hammerbacher, J. (2009). *Beautiful data*. O'Reilly.

Tabachnick, B. G., & Fidell, L. S. (2018). *Using multivariate statistics* (7th ed.). Pearson.

Yin, R. (1998). *Dynamic learning patterns during individualized instruction* [Unpublished doctoral dissertation]. Indiana University Graduate School.

2 Overview of the Big Study

Summary: We apply APT to a large-scale study of the effectiveness of First Principles of Instruction within the online Indiana University Plagiarism Tutorials and Tests (IPTAT). We begin by illustrating two typical cases of learning journeys: Sam and Melinda. We next summarize the results from our Big Study of over 936,000 learning journeys during 2019 and 2020. We demonstrate how we found that, on average in each learning journey, successful students were nearly four times more likely to utilize unique parts of IPTAT which were designed with First Principles of Instruction, when compared with unsuccessful students.

A Tale of Two Learning Journeys

Learning Journey #1: Sam's Case

Early Tuesday morning on October 6, 2020, Sam (pseudonym) started to work on his assignment for his writing class for first-year college students. His instructor expects students in this freshmen composition course to pass an online test on how to recognize plagiarism. Sam is sitting in his favorite chair with his laptop computer. Imagine that we are standing behind the chair, looking over Sam's shoulder at what he is doing on his laptop. He opens his Safari web browser and does a Google search for "Indiana University plagiarism tutorial and test". He sees a link on the search results, "How to Recognize Plagiarism—Indiana University", and clicks on it. The first thing he sees on his display is illustrated in Figure 2.1. He takes a minute to read through the Welcome page, ignoring the movie about Dr. Leftwich and Grace.

Since his goal is to pass a Certification Test, Sam immediately decides to take one to see what it is like. He clicks on the link in the sidebar to "Take Certification Tests". The rest of Sam's early morning learning journey is temporally listed in Map 2.1 sequentially, pageview by pageview. If we had made a video recording, then each row of Map 2.1 could be used as a

DOI: 10.4324/9781003176343-02

10   Overview of the Big Study

Figure 2.1 Screenshot of IPTAT "Welcome" Page in 2020

Overview of the Big Study 11

subtitle superimposed on the video in real-time, similar to closed captioning. Column 1 instead shows thumbnail images of IPTAT webpages that Sam visited. You could largely re-enact Sam's temporal map yourself by clicking on links, starting at https://plagiarism.iu.edu.

Each time Sam sees a different web page in his browser, a new row is created in Map 2.1. Each row shows the time in column 2, a sequence number in

Map 2.1 Temporal Map for IPTAT User Sam

User View	Time	#	Web Page URL at https://plagiarism.iu.edu	Page: User Action
	06:21:32 a.m.	1	/index.html	IPTAT Welcome: selects "Take Certification Tests".
	06:22:28 a.m.	2	/certificationTests/index.html	Take Certification Test: selects "Undergraduate and Advance High School Student".
	06:22:35 a.m.	3	/mainLogin.php	Login for Certification Test: selects link to register.
	06:22:37 a.m.	4	/register.html	Register for Certification Test: selects link "I am an undergraduate …".
	06:22:48 a.m.	5	/mainLogin.php?action=register&testLevel=UG	Register as an Undergraduate … : completes form and submits it.
	06:25:41 a.m.	6	/mainLogin.php?action=registration&testLevel=UG	IPTAT Instructions: Go to your e-mail now.
	No Google Analytics event stored	--	E-mail app, not IPTAT	User reads e-mail and selects link to confirm registration.
	06:27:47 a.m.	7	/mainLogin.php?action=activate&testLevel=UG	Registration is activated: logs in to take UG test.
	06:27:58 a.m.	8	/plagiarismTestUG.php?testLevel=UG (One of trillions of randomized Certification Tests)	Takes test and submits it for evaluation.
	06:33:18 a.m.	9	/evaluateAnswersTestUG.php	UG Test Evaluation: user does not pass, clicks on first link for type of plagiarism.

(*Continued*)

12 Overview of the Big Study

Map 2.1 (Continued)

	06:34:56 a.m.	10	/plagiarismPatterns/patternCunningCoverUp.html	Plagiarism Pattern: user missed a Cunning Cover-Up question. Selects back button on browser.
	06:35:22 a.m.	11	/evaluateAnswersTestUG.php	Returns to UG Test Evaluation: clicks on next link for type of plagiarism.
	06:35:25 a.m.	12	/plagiarismPatterns/patternDeceptiveDupe.html	Plagiarism Pattern: user missed a Deceptive Dupe question. Selects back button on browser.
	06:37:01 a.m.	13	/evaluateAnswersTestUG.php	Returns to UG Test Evaluation: clicks on button "Learn how to recognize plagiarism".
	06:37:21 a.m.	14	/index.html	Returns to Welcome Page: user decides to quit for now, and plans to come back later. Closes browser window.

Note that Sam did not pass a Certification Test. This is an unsuccessful learning journey on October 6, 2020.

column 3, and the web page URL (address) in column 4. Column 5 describes what Sam did. If we were constructing the APT temporal map of Sam's learning journey through IPTAT, we would just write down the times and web page URLs as shown in columns two and four. The extra information provided here in columns 1, 3, and 5 is to help you better understand the map.

Map 2.1 shows that Sam's learning journey was relatively short, beginning at 6:21 a.m. and ending at 6:37 a.m., during which he viewed 14 IPTAT pages. His learning journey lasted about 16 minutes overall. In essence, Sam registered to take a Certification Test and immediately took one, which he did not pass on his first attempt. On the test results page, there were four links to types of questions he missed. He clicked on the first two links, respectively, and saw examples of questions similar to those he missed on the test. He then clicked on the button to "learn how to recognize plagiarism" which returned him to the Welcome page. Sam concludes that he'll need to spend more time later, since he needs to eat breakfast and get going to his 8 a.m. class.

We consider Sam's learning journey as unsuccessful in that he did not pass a Certification Test. If he had, Map 2.1 would contain a link to https://plagiarism.iu.edu/mailCertificateUG.php. This PHP page/script can *only* be accessed immediately after a user passes a Certification Test.

Learning Journey #2: Melinda's Case

Like Sam, Melinda (pseudonym) is also an undergraduate student. She started on the Certification Test page on Sunday evening, October 4, 2020, at 5:53 p.m., but then navigated immediately to the Welcome page at 5:54 p.m. She spent about 79 minutes in her first session, then took a break.

Map 2.2 Temporal Map of Session 1 for IPTAT User Melinda

Time	Web Page HTML Title	Web Page URL at https://plagiarism.iu.edu
5:53 p.m.	Certification Tests	/certificationTests/index.html
5:54 p.m.	Welcome	/index.html
5:54 p.m.	Certification Tests	/certificationTests/index.html
6:01 p.m.	Welcome	/index.html
6:05 p.m.	Organization of Instruction	/organization.html
6:06 p.m.	How to Navigate	/navigation.html
6:06 p.m.	Overview	/overview/index.html
6:07 p.m.	What you should do	/overview/shouldDo.html
6:08 p.m.	But I won't get caught	/overview/easyDetection.html
6:10 p.m.	R U a dupe?	/overview/RUAdupe.html
6:14 p.m.	The Slippery Slope with Symbolic Signs	/overview/signs.html
6:29 p.m.	Cases of Plagiarism	/overview/cases.html
6:33 p.m.	Tutorials and Practice Tests	/tutorials/index.html
6:33 p.m.	Task 1 Overview	/tutorials/task1/index.html
6:37 p.m.	A Video Case	/tutorials/task1/activation.html
6:44 p.m.	Demonstration	/tutorials/task1/demonstration.html
6:47 p.m.	Demonstration Continued	/tutorials/task1/demonstration2.html
6:50 p.m.	Practice with One Item at a Time	/practiceTest.php?task=1&item=1
6:51 p.m.	Practice Question Result and Feedback	/practiceTestResults.php
6:51 p.m.	Practice with One Item at a Time	/practiceTest.php?task=1&item=2
6:52 p.m.	Practice Question Result and Feedback	/practiceTestResults.php
6:52 p.m.	Practice with One Item at a Time	/practiceTest.php?task=1&item=3
6:52 p.m.	Practice Question Result and Feedback	/practiceTestResults.php
6:53 p.m.	Practice with One Item at a Time	/practiceTest.php?task=1&item=4
6:53 p.m.	Practice Question Result and Feedback	/practiceTestResults.php
6:53 p.m.	Task 1 Integration	/tutorials/task1/integration.html
6:56 p.m.	Practice Test 1	/tutorials/task1/masteryTest.php
6:59 p.m.	Practice Test 1 Feedback	/tutorials/task1/masteryTestResults.php
6:59 p.m.	Task 2 Overview	/tutorials/task2/index.html
7:00 p.m.	Task 2 Activation, A Video Case	/tutorials/task2/activation.html

(*Continued*)

14 Overview of the Big Study

Map 2.2 (Continued)

Time	Web Page HTML Title	Web Page URL at https://plagiarism.iu.edu
7:01 p.m.	Task 2 Demonstration	/tutorials/task2/demonstration.html
7:08 p.m.	Practice with One Item at a Time	/practiceTest.php?task=2&item=1
7:08 p.m.	Practice Question Result and Feedback	/practiceTestResults.php
7:09 p.m.	Practice with One Item at a Time	/practiceTest.php?task=2&item=2
7:09 p.m.	Practice Question Result and Feedback	/practiceTestResults.php
7:09 p.m.	Practice with One Item at a Time	/practiceTest.php?task=2&item=3
7:10 p.m.	Practice Question Result and Feedback	/practiceTestResults.php
7:10 p.m.	Practice with One Item at a Time	/practiceTest.php?task=2&item=4
7:10 p.m.	Practice Question Result and Feedback	/practiceTestResults.php
7:10 p.m.	Task 2 Integration	/tutorials/task2/integration.html
7:11 p.m.	Practice Test 2	/tutorials/task2/masteryTest.php
7:12 p.m.	Practice Test 2 Feedback	/tutorials/task2/masteryTestResults.php
7:12 p.m.	Task 3 Overview	/tutorials/task3/index.html

Note: Duration is ~79 minutes on October 4, 2020.

At 8:03 p.m., she began session 2 of her IPTAT learning journey and spent about 69 more minutes until she passed a Certification Test. Her learning journey lasted nearly 148 minutes in total, split across two sessions separated by a break of about 52 minutes.

Melinda spent most of her time doing all five tutorials and practice tests before she registered to take a Certification Test. As you can see in Map 2.3, she activated her IPTAT registration at 8:54 p.m. and then took a Certification Test. She viewed the 'hints.html' web page while taking the test, which summarizes the logic for classifying the student version as word-for-word plagiarism, paraphrasing plagiarism, and non-plagiarism. She viewed the evaluation of her test answers at 9:06 p.m. At 9:12 p.m., she clicked on the button to mail her Certificate (https://plagiarism.iu.edu/mailCertificateUG.php), so she must have just passed a test, since IPTAT will not execute this script unless a Certification Test is passed *and* the student clicks on the button on the test results page to mail their Certificate to the e-mail address they used when registering for IPTAT. The Certificate contains information on which test was passed, her name, and information about the test passed that includes the IP address of the computing device used, the unique Test ID, and how long the test took. Melinda can forward this e-mail to her teacher, and she can save her Certificate as a PDF file and upload it to the drop box for her class.

Map 2.3 Temporal Map of Session 2 for User Melinda

Time	Web Page HTML Title	Web Page URL at https://plagiarism.iu.edu
8:03 p.m.	Task 3 Activation, A Video Case	/tutorials/task3/activation.html
8:04 p.m.	Task 3 Demonstration	/tutorials/task3/demonstration.html
8:09 p.m.	Practice with One Item at a Time	/practiceTest.php?task=3&item=1
8:09 p.m.	Practice Question Result and Feedback	/practiceTestResults.php
8:09 p.m.	Practice with One Item at a Time	/practiceTest.php?task=3&item=2
8:09 p.m.	Practice Question Result and Feedback	/practiceTestResults.php
8:10 p.m.	Practice with One Item at a Time	/practiceTest.php?task=3&item=3
8:10 p.m.	Practice Question Result and Feedback	/practiceTestResults.php
8:10 p.m.	Practice with One Item at a Time	/practiceTest.php?task=3&item=4
8:10 p.m.	Practice Question Result and Feedback	/practiceTestResults.php
8:10 p.m.	Task 3 Integration	/tutorials/task3/integration.html
8:11 p.m.	Practice Test 3	/tutorials/task3/masteryTest.php
8:11 p.m.	Practice Test 3 Feedback	/tutorials/task3/masteryTestResults.php
8:11 p.m.	Task 4 Overview	/tutorials/task4/index.html
8:12 p.m.	Task 4 Activation, Video Case 1	/tutorials/task4/activation.html
8:14 p.m.	Task 4 Activation Video Case 2	/tutorials/task4/activation2.html
8:17 p.m.	Task 4 Demonstration	/tutorials/task4/demonstration.html
8:24 p.m.	Practice with One Item at a Time	/practiceTest.php?task=4&item=1
8:24 p.m.	Practice Question Result and Feedback	/practiceTestResults.php
8:24 p.m.	Practice with One Item at a Time	/practiceTest.php?task=4&item=2
8:24 p.m.	Practice Question Result and Feedback	/practiceTestResults.php
8:24 p.m.	Practice with One Item at a Time	/practiceTest.php?task=4&item=3
8:24 p.m.	Practice Question Result and Feedback	/practiceTestResults.php
8:24 p.m.	Practice with One Item at a Time	/practiceTest.php?task=4&item=4
8:25 p.m.	Practice Question Result and Feedback	/practiceTestResults.php
8:25 p.m.	Practice with One Item at a Time	/practiceTest.php?task=4&item=5
8:26 p.m.	Practice Question Result and Feedback	/practiceTestResults.php
8:26 p.m.	Practice with One Item at a Time	/practiceTest.php?task=4&item=6
8:27 p.m.	Practice Question Result and Feedback	/practiceTestResults.php
8:27 p.m.	Practice with One Item at a Time	/practiceTest.php?task=4&item=7
8:27 p.m.	Practice Question Result and Feedback	/practiceTestResults.php
8:27 p.m.	Practice with One Item at a Time	/practiceTest.php?task=4&item=8

(*Continued*)

Overview of the Big Study

Map 2.3 (Continued)

Time	Web Page HTML Title	Web Page URL at https://plagiarism.iu.edu
8:27 p.m.	Practice Question Result and Feedback	/practiceTestResults.php
8:27 p.m.	Task 4 Integration	/tutorials/task4/integration.html
8:28 p.m.	Practice Test 4	/tutorials/task4/masteryTest.php
8:30 p.m.	Practice Test 4 Feedback	/tutorials/task4/masteryTestResults.php
8:30 p.m.	Task 5 Overview	/tutorials/task5/index.html
8:31 p.m.	Task 5 Activation, Video Case 1	/tutorials/task5/activation.html
8:32 p.m.	Task 5 Activation, Video Case 2	/tutorials/task5/activation2.html
8:33 p.m.	Task 5 Activation, Video Case 3	/tutorials/task5/activation3.html
8:34 p.m.	Task 5 Demonstration	/tutorials/task5/demonstration.html
8:42 p.m.	Practice with One Item at a Time	/practiceTest.php?task=5&item=1
8:43 p.m.	Practice Question Result and Feedback	/practiceTestResults.php
8:43 p.m.	Practice with One Item at a Time	/practiceTest.php?task=5&item=2
8:44 p.m.	Practice Question Result and Feedback	/practiceTestResults.php
8:44 p.m.	Practice with One Item at a Time	/practiceTest.php?task=5&item=3
8:44 p.m.	Practice Question Result and Feedback	/practiceTestResults.php
8:44 p.m.	Practice with One Item at a Time	/practiceTest.php?task=5&item=4
8:45 p.m.	Practice Question Result and Feedback	/practiceTestResults.php
8:45 p.m.	Practice with One Item at a Time	/practiceTest.php?task=5&item=5
8:46 p.m.	Practice Question Result and Feedback	/practiceTestResults.php
8:47 p.m.	Practice with One Item at a Time	/practiceTest.php?task=5&item=6
8:47 p.m.	Practice Question Result and Feedback	/practiceTestResults.php
8:47 p.m.	Practice with One Item at a Time	/practiceTest.php?task=5&item=7
8:47 p.m.	Practice Question Result and Feedback	/practiceTestResults.php
8:47 p.m.	Practice with One Item at a Time	/practiceTest.php?task=5&item=8
8:47 p.m.	Practice Question Result and Feedback	/practiceTestResults.php
8:48 p.m.	Practice with One Item at a Time	/practiceTest.php?task=5&item=9
8:48 p.m.	Practice Question Result and Feedback	/practiceTestResults.php
8:48 p.m.	Practice with One Item at a Time	/practiceTest.php?task=5&item=10
8:48 p.m.	Practice Question Result and Feedback	/practiceTestResults.php
8:48 p.m.	Task 5 Integration	/tutorials/task5/integration.html
8:50 p.m.	Practice Test 5	/tutorials/task5/masteryTest.php
8:52 p.m.	Practice Test 5 Feedback	/tutorials/task5/masteryTestResults.php

Map 2.3 (Continued)

Time	Web Page HTML Title	Web Page URL at https://plagiarism.iu.edu
8:52 p.m.	Register	/register.html
8:52 p.m.	Authentication Dialogue	/mainLogin.php?action=register&testLevel=UG
8:54 p.m.	Authentication Dialogue	/mainLogin.php?action=activate&testLevel=UG
8:54 p.m.	Undergraduate Certification Tests	/plagiarismTestUG.php?testLevel=UG
8:56 p.m.	Hints	/hints.html
9:06 p.m.	Undergraduate Certification Test Evaluation	/evaluateAnswersTestUG.php
9:10 p.m.	Hints	/hints.html
9:12 p.m.	Mail Certificate	/mailCertificateUG.php

Note: Duration is ~69 Minutes. This is a successful learning journey, because she passed a Certification Test and mailed her Certificate at 9:12 p.m. on October 4, 2020 at the IPTAT website.

How do we know all this about Melinda's learning journey? Google Analytics (GA) was tracking her interaction with the IPTAT website. We later used the Universal Analytics (UA) tool to generate an Audience report during the first two weeks of October. Within the Audience tool, we selected the User Explorer tool, where we selected a user at random, by skipping to the 10,000th case when viewing cases in descending order of the number of sessions.

Actually, GA doesn't know that it's Melinda, nor do we from the GA tracking; GA stores only the client ID of the device she is using: 2134533298.1601848429. GA further stores the web location of the client referral as 'ung.view.usg.edu' (which is the online learning management system at the University of Northern Georgia), and we can infer that Melinda clicked on a link provided most likely by her instructor, which took her directly to the Certification Test page that she viewed at the beginning of session 1.

We are using pseudonyms here for Melinda and Sam, and when doing APT we are focusing solely on their interaction with IPTAT. In Chapters 3 and 4 we present aggregate information about who uses IPTAT, but we do not provide information about specific users that will identify them, as a matter of protecting their individual privacy (see https://plagiarism.iu.edu/privacy.html). Noteworthy is that learning journeys for these two sample cases are similar to those from hundreds of thousands of IPTAT users.

Sam experienced a different learning journey than Melinda, an unsuccessful one at that. His journey consisted of one session that lasted about 16 minutes, whereas Melinda's two sessions lasted nearly 2.5 hours in total. We consider Melinda's learning journey as successful, since she passed a

Certification Test. We know this because the last pageview in her Google Analytics session 2 executed the script at https://plagiarism.iu.edu/mail CertificateUG.php. Sam's learning journey did not have such a pageview.

Design and Structure of IPTAT Using First Principles of Instruction

We provide more detail about the design of IPTAT in Chapter 3. Here we outline the overall organization. From Melinda's Maps 2.2 and 2.3, we can see that she viewed web pages in sequence, by clicking on the *next page* links, whereas Sam navigated directly to the Certification Tests index page, registered, logged in, and took a test. While students are free to navigate IPTAT however they choose, we focus on Melinda's maps since they illustrate the organization.

Problem-Centered Principle

The tutorials are organized by five levels, from Basic to Expert. These illustrate one of the First Principles of Instruction (FPI), the *problem-centered principle*, which is to provide students with a sequence of authentic problems or tasks, organized from simple to complex. Within each task level, there are further IPTAT web pages designed with the remaining four principles: activation, demonstration, application, and integration.

For example, in Melinda's Maps 2.2 and 2.3, she viewed the '/tutorials/task1/index.html' page at 6:33 p.m. This page describes the basic difference between committing plagiarism and avoiding it. Four minutes later, at 6:37 p.m. she viewed '/tutorials/task1/activation.html'. This web page was designed with the FPI activation principle, as can be seen in Map 2.2 at 6:37 p.m. This page provides a one-minute video case, which is followed by the IU definition of plagiarism. We refer to the simplest level of the problem as Task 1 here, and the most complex as Task 5. Map 2.2 indicates that Melinda began Task 2 at 6:59 p.m., and Task 3 at 7:12 p.m. After her break, she continued with Task 3. At 8:11 p.m. she began Task 4, and at 8:30 p.m. she began Task 5.

In other words, Melinda did the tutorials and tasks in the order designed, from simple to more complex levels of classifying examples of plagiarism as either word-for-word or paraphrasing plagiarism, or as non-plagiarism.

Activation Principle

The *activation principle* prescribes helping students connect what they already know or believe with what they will be newly learning. Merrill (2020) describes the *activation principle* as follows: "Learning is promoted when learners activate a mental model of their prior knowledge and skill as a foundation for new skills" (p. 2). Maps 2.2 and 2.3 indicate that Melinda viewed web pages which were designed using the activation principle at 6:37, 7:00, 8:03, 8:12, 8:14, 8:31, 8:32, and 8:33 p.m. We refer to these pages as "Video Cases" in IPTAT, since we do not expect students to know the terminology Merrill uses for FPI.

There are a total of eight pages in the tutorials which are designed with the activation principle.

Demonstration Principle

We utilized the FPI *demonstration principle* by making screencasts of a person writing a paper and talking about what they are doing. At each task level, the demonstrations provide a dynamic view of the writing process, so the user can see concrete examples of plagiarism and especially how to correct it by creating proper quotations and paraphrases, appropriate citations, and bibliographic references. Merrill (2020) states the *demonstration principle*: "Learning is promoted when learners observe a demonstration of the knowledge and skill to be learned that is consistent with the type of skill being taught" (p. 1). Thus, IPTAT not only tells students what plagiarism is and is not, but also *shows* them—by providing dynamic examples.

In Maps 2.2 and 2.3, we can see that Melinda viewed pages designed with the *demonstration principle* at 6:44, 6:47, 7:01, 8:04, and 8:17 p.m., a total of five such web pages.

Application Principle

Merrill (2020) describes the *application principle*: "Learning is promoted when learners engage in the application of their newly acquired knowledge and skill that is consistent with the type of skill being taught" (p. 1). Furthermore, as students try themselves to do the task or solve the problem, it is important to provide feedback which is intrinsic or corrective; and coaching can provide further guidance as needed. We designed a series of practice items in IPTAT that are structured to be consistent with test items they will later encounter on Certification Tests. For example, in Map 2.1, you can see that Melinda did all four practice items at the Basic Level (Task 1), starting at 6:50 p.m. After each item, IPTAT provides the student with feedback on their answer.

IPTAT contains a total of 30 web pages designed with the *application principle*. We refer to these as "practice questions" in IPTAT.

Integration Principle

The idea of the *integration principle* is that students can incorporate what they have learned into their own lives. In other words, they actually use what they have learned. In the case of learning to avoid plagiarism by being able to identify it, the best form of integration would likely be to ask students to write papers or make speeches and observe whether or not they plagiarize. This was not practical in designing IPTAT, since there are no live instructors to judge student *integration*, and it would have been extremely difficult for us to design software that might try to emulate human judgements of plagiarism.

Merrill (2020) states the *integration principle*: "Learning is promoted when learners reflect on, discuss, and defend their newly acquired knowledge and skill" (p. 2). We decided to design *integration* web pages by asking students to type in a text box their reflections about what they had just learned at each task level. We did not design IPTAT software to provide feedback or comments on student reflections, although we do store the text of their reflections for future analysis.

There are a total of five web pages in the IPTAT tutorials which we designed with the *integration principle*, and which Melinda viewed at 6:53, 7:10, 8:10, 8:27, and 8:48 p.m.

Table 2.1 summarizes the organization of IPAT according to First Principles of Instruction.

Results from 936,417 Learning Journeys through IPTAT in the Big Study in 2019 and 2020

Chapter 4 describes in more detail how we arrived at these results. We provide the big picture here, so you can see the overall benefits of doing APT of learning journeys.

Tables 2.2 and 2.3 summarize results for learning journeys of IPTAT users between January 1, 2019 and December 31, 2020. During this two-year temporal window, we have Google Analytics records of learning journeys. We have classified journeys in which a Certification Test was passed as successful. There were 300,333 such Certificant learning journeys during this temporal window. On the other hand, there are 636,084 learning journeys for Non-Certificants, who did not pass a Certification Test during their journeys. Overall, there are 936,417 learning journeys reported in the Big Study.

Table 2.3 shows summary statistics for temporal patterns, which were counted within 1,866,387 temporal maps. These maps contain a total of 36,443,455 pageviews of the IPTAT website during the two-year temporal window. Each learning journey consists of one or more temporal maps. Each temporal map contains a sequence of IPTAT pageviews with date/time stamps in which the time between pageviews was less than 30 minutes. For example, Melinda's learning journey is described by two temporal maps, since she took a 52-minute break between sessions.

Overview of the Big Study 21

Table 2.1 IPTAT Big Study: Structure of Tutorials and Tests Designed with First Principles of Instruction

Task Level	Level Name	First Principle	Pages/ Instances	Page URLs at https:// plagiarism.iu.edu
1	Basic	Activation	1/1	/tutorials/task1/activation.html
		Demonstration	2/4	/tutorials/task1/demonstration.html
				/tutorials/task1/demonstration2.html
		Application	4/4	/practiceTest.php?task=1&item=1...4
		Integration	1/1	/tutorials/task1/integration.html
		Practice Test	1/4	/tutorials/task1/masteryTest.php
2	Novice	Activation	1/1	/tutorials/task2/activation.html
		Demonstration	1/2	/tutorials/task2/demonstration.html
		Application	4/4	/practiceTest.php?task=2&item=1...4
		Integration	1/1	/tutorials/task2/integration.html
		Practice Test	1/4	/tutorials /task2/masteryTest.php
3	Intermediate	Activation	1/1	/tutorials/task3/activation.html
		Demonstration	1/2	/tutorials/task3/demonstration.html
		Application	4/4	/practiceTest.php?task=3&item=1...4
		Integration	1/1	/tutorials/task3/integration.html
		Practice Test	1/4	/tutorials /task3/masteryTest.php
4	Advanced	Activation	2/2	/tutorials/task4/activation.html
				/tutorials/task4/activation2.html
		Demonstration	1/2	/tutorials/task4/demonstration.html
		Application	8/8	/practiceTest.php?task=4&item=1...8
		Integration	1/1	/tutorials/task4/integration.html
		Practice Test	1/8	/tutorials /task4/masteryTest.php
5	Expert	Activation	3/3	/tutorials/task5/activation.html
				/tutorials/task5/activation2.html
				/tutorials/task5/activation3.html
		Demonstration	1/2	/tutorials/task5/demonstration.html
		Application	10/10	/practiceTest.php?task=5&item=1...10
		Integration	1/1	/tutorials/task5/integration.html
		Practice Test	1/10	/tutorials /task4/masteryTest.php
All	Undergrad	Certification	1/10	/plagiarismTestUG.php
	Graduate	Tests (trillions)	1/10	/plagiarismTestGR.php
	Undergrad	Test Feedback	1	/evaluateAnswersTestUG.php
	Graduate		1	/evaluateAnswersTestGR.php

(*Continued*)

Table 2.1 (Continued)

Task Level	Level Name	First Principle	Pages/ Instances	Page URLs at https:// plagiarism.iu.edu
All	Plagiarism Patterns	Adaptive Demonstration	1/18	/plagiarismPatterns/...
All		Activate Registration	1/1	/mainLogin.php?action=activate...
	Undergrad	Mail Certificate	1	/mailCertificateUG.php
	Graduate		1	/mailCertificateGR.php
All	Overview	Activation	1/6	/overview/...
All	Welcome	Activation	1/1	/index.html

Table 2.2 Google Analytics Data on IPTAT Usage: Big Study 2019–2020

	Total	Certificants	Non-Certificants
Learning Journeys	936,417	300,333	636,084
Mean number of sessions per learning journey per Google Analytics client	1.99	2.71	1.65

How did we get so much data? And how did we obtain these results? We provide more details in Chapter 4 about how we derived the APT results shown in Table 2.3 and Figure 2.2.

Activation Results

Certificants viewed, on average, 7.45 unique activation pages per journey. A web page can be viewed more than once during a session, but it is counted only once—that's what a unique pageview is. Thus, Certificants on average viewed nearly all of the activation pages in the tutorials, whereas Non-Certificants viewed on average 2.03 pages designed with the *activation principle*. Thus, Certificants were 3.67 times more likely to view IPTAT activation pages than were Non-Certificants (7.45 divided by 2.03).

When we designed the IPTAT tutorials in 2015, we implemented the FPI *activation principle* by creating video cases, as a way to prime students for what they will be learning. Since IPTAT students would be accessing IPTAT over the Web from around the world, we decided to provide a common experience to relate to, albeit vicarious—real people who are confronted with having committed plagiarism, often out of ignorance or misunderstanding of the finer nuances of plagiarism, and how they deal with their issues. These brief videos further illustrate constructive ways that students

Overview of the Big Study   23

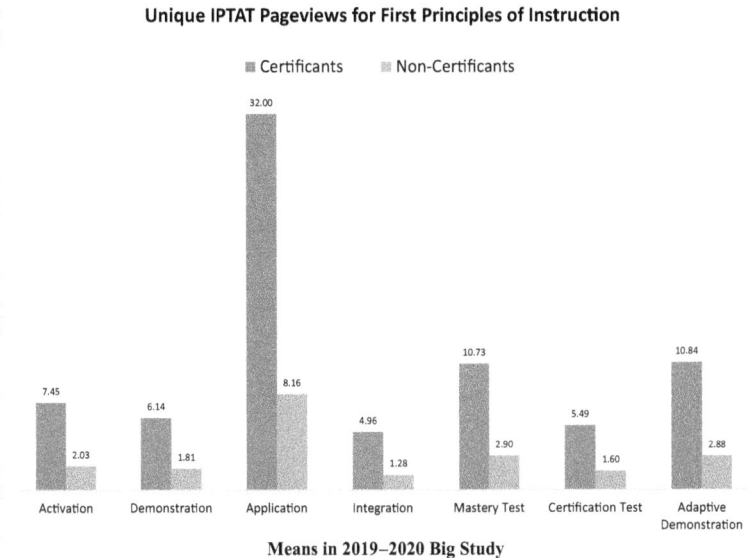

Figure 2.2 Mean Unique Pageviews for Certificants and Non-Certificants in the Big Study

can subsequently avoid plagiarizing by fixing it in their own writing, often facilitated by their teacher or by a knowledgeable peer.

Demonstration Results

In Table 2.1, you can see in the second row that there are two unique *demonstration* pages at the Basic Level, and each of these provides two screencasts. Overall, we provide six unique *demonstration* pages, as can be seen in Table 2.1. In Table 2.3, in the second row, note that Certificants viewed, on average, 6.14 unique *demonstration* pages, whereas Non-Certificants viewed a mean of 1.81, for an odds ratio of 3.40. How can Certificants (or even Non-Certificants) view more than six unique pages? Because their learning journeys often have more than one temporal map (or session). As can be seen in Table 2.2, Certificants have 2.71 sessions per learning journey on average, and uniqueness of pageviews is determined by Google Analytics as *within* sessions. For example, Melinda's learning journey was split into two sessions separated by a 52-minute break. She could have viewed '/tutorials/task2/demonstration.html' three different times in her first session, and then viewed the same page once again in the second session. If

24 Overview of the Big Study

Table 2.3 Temporal Patterns per Learning Journey (n = 936,417 Journeys): Big Study 2019–2020

First Principle of Instruction or Activity	Maximum Possible Unique Pages in IPTAT	Certificants: Mean Unique Pageviews	Non-Certificants: Mean Unique Pageviews	Odds Ratio (Certificants to Non-Certificants)
Activation	8	7.45	2.03	3.67
Demonstration	6	6.14	1.81	3.40
Application	30	32.00	8.16	3.92
Integration	5	4.96	1.28	3.87
Practice Test	5	10.73	2.90	3.70
Certification Test Evaluations	1	5.49	1.60	3.42
Plagiarism Patterns	19	10.84	2.88	3.77
All First Principles	74	77.60	20.65	3.76
Time Spent (H:MM:SS)	~	1:37:59	0:21:37	4.53

she had done so, Google Analytics would count this as two unique views of web pages that we designed by implementing the *demonstration principle*.

Thus, a unique pageview is in actuality the number of separate *sessions* (i.e., APT temporal maps) in which that particular web page is viewed at least once. While this may be confusing, this is how Google Analytics determines unique pageviews, which is based on their definition of a session. The alternative would be to count total views of each page within a learning journey, which we could do also. However, when a user clicks on the browser's "back" button, this counts that same page twice, once when it is first viewed, and again when it is displayed a second time via navigating backwards. We believe that unique pageviews (session counts) are a better gauge for characterizing learning journeys because of the way the Web and web browsers work. The browser's back button is a way for the user to navigate to the previous page, often in order to click on a different hyperlink, rather than rereading that previous page carefully a second time.

Application Principle

Notice in Table 2.1 that, in the third row, the *application principle* is utilized on four different IPTAT web pages, for a total of four items. And note that in Table 2.1 there are 30 unique practice items implemented across the five task levels in IPTAT tutorials. Certificants on average viewed 32.00 unique web pages designed with the *application principle*, compared with 8.16 unique pageviews by Non-Certificants. (See above explanation of counting unique pageviews and sessions.)

Integration Principle

You can see in Table 2.1 in the fourth row the *integration principle* is instantiated at the Basic Level by one page, '/tutorials/task1/integration.html' and that there are five total web pages designed for the *integration principle* in the tutorials. In Table 2.3, notice that the average number of unique *integration* pageviews by Certificants is 4.96 per learning journey, whereas the mean is 1.28 for Non-Certificants per learning journey.

Overall Unique Pageviews

In Table 2.3, note that Certificants viewed, on average, 77.60 web pages per learning journey. Non-Certificants viewed 20.65 pages per journey. Overall, Certificants viewed 3.76 times as many unique IPTAT web pages, when compared with Non-Certificants. Since there are 74 unique FPI pages, Certificants viewed, on average, some of the same FPI pages in different GA sessions.

Certificants also spent about 4.53 times longer viewing IPTAT web pages on average in their learning journeys. Certificants spent about 98 minutes, whereas Non-Certificants spent about 22 minutes on average per journey.

What Does All This Mean?

Successful students, who passed one of the difficult IPTAT Certification Tests, spent over four times as much time interacting with IPTAT than did unsuccessful students, and viewed nearly four times as many unique IPTAT web pages that we designed with First Principles of Instruction.

We also know from our own record keeping at IU, not from Google Analytics, how many students activated their IPTAT registrations, and of those, how many passed a Certification Test. We discuss this in detail in Chapters 3 and 4. The overall success rate is 81 percent. This means that about four out of every five students who use IPTAT do eventually pass a Certification Test. We do not have records at IU on students who never attempt to register for IPTAT, whereas Google Analytics tracks users whether they are registered or not.

There are many users, such as in Melinda's case, who spend considerable time learning via the IPTAT tutorials and then register for Certification Tests. And there are other users, such as in Sam's case, who register for a Certification Test but do few or no tutorials, according to Google Analytics records. If they never pass a test during the temporal window in which we observe them, then they are a Non-Certificant in our IU records.

But many students, similar to Sam's case, will return later and use more of our IPTAT resources. If Sam were to visit IPTAT initially on one device and browser (such as his laptop computer) and later to visit using a different device and browser (such as on his smartphone), and yet a third time on a desktop machine in a school computer lab, these will be identified as Google Analytics sessions with different client IDs. This is a limitation of Google Analytics unless additional information about user identity is tracked. We discuss this issue in greater detail in Chapter 4.

Additionally, some users may set their devices to prevent tracking of browser usage (e.g., in their settings of browser preferences, by disabling Javascript, by incognito browsing, or by using anti-malware programs which prevent trackers). In these situations, Google Analytics sessions may not be recorded at all.

Furthermore, Google Analytics can't normally "see" who is using the device when tracking users. If devices are shared among students, such as computers in school labs or among family members at home, when a different person uses the same computer and browser Google Analytics may not be able to tell that it is a different person, since the client ID could be the same.

These situations do add some noise to our IPTAT findings, since there is no practical way we can unambiguously detect all of these different circumstances. Nonetheless, as we discuss in Chapter 4, the millions of temporal patterns within IPTAT learning journeys are highly consistent from quarter to quarter over two years, and also consistent with data we collected earlier between 2016 and 2019 (not reported here). Two facts are apparent:

1. Many students use more than one digital device to access the Internet and the Web, such as a smartphone and a laptop or desktop computer.
2. Until the learning journey in which a student does pass a Certification test, if there are any earlier learning journeys on different devices, those previous learning journeys will be classified as Non-Certificant journeys.

However, think about this. This pattern of first being unsuccessful while trying to learn, followed later by success, is typically the case for new student learning. It is not uncommon for a student to try and fail a number of times before a new skill or body of knowledge is mastered. First a student is unsuccessful, and then after some time of trying to learn, they can succeed and hence achieve their goal. As we discussed with the Oregon Trail metaphor at the beginning of Chapter 1, not everyone who attempted the journey arrived at their destination. And until they get there, they have not yet arrived. Would they eventually? We don't know while they are still on the trip, unless of course they die or drop out for other reasons.

In the case of IPTAT, we do know from our own records at IU (independent from Google Analytics tracking data) that 81 percent of registrants succeed by passing a Certification Test. This percentage has remained relatively stable since 2016. The tests are not easy to pass. They cannot be passed solely by guessing, and our test logs indicate that, overall, one in seven tests is passed. There are trillions of combinations of unique, timed Certification Tests, each consisting of ten randomly selected questions from large inventories. Sophisticated algorithms make it extremely difficult and onerous to cheat by using answer keys. Instructors can further validate Certificates to make sure they are not counterfeit.

We further know that student learning journeys that end in success, on average, include three to four times as much interaction with web pages that were designed with First Principles of Instruction, when compared with student learning journeys which have not been successful (at least thus far).

Student persistence and effort matter. First Principles of Instruction matter, too. It's no accident that 315,424 registrants passed an IPTAT Certification Test in 2019 and 2020. These students were from 213 countries and territories worldwide, mostly ranging in age between 14 and 44. When we use a longer time frame, from 2016 through 2020, IPTAT records indicate that 749,989 registered users passed an IPTAT Certification Test. GA Audience reports indicate that users were from 225 countries and territories worldwide during the same five-year interval. These big data support the overall generalizability about the effectiveness of First Principles of Instruction as implemented in the Indiana University Plagiarism Tutorials and Tests.

Chapters 3 and 4 provide more details about these findings.

We hope that this book provides a roadmap for how you and others can evaluate effectiveness of online instruction and learning. When you are finished with this book, you should have learned enough so that when you design your own instructional website, you will have at your fingertips an easy-to-understand but powerful way to determine its effectiveness. You should also be able to investigate the effectiveness of *different* design principles and instructional strategies—by following the same approach as we have illustrated in this book for *First Principles of Instruction*.

References

Merrill, M. D. (2020). *M. David Merrill's first principles of instruction*. Association for Educational Communications and Technology.

3 The Indiana University Plagiarism Tutorials and Tests
2002 through 2020

Summary: We describe how we redesigned the IPTAT in 2015 using First Principles of Instruction. We provide examples of IPTAT web pages and learning activities that illustrate FPI: sequencing tasks from simple to complex; activation of prior knowledge; demonstration of skills to be learned; application of newly acquired skills to solve problems; and integration of new skills in one's everyday life. We also describe how we created trillions of Certification Tests to measure student success in classifying word-for-word, paraphrasing, and non-plagiarism when viewing original source materials and samples of student writing. We conclude by describing two years of IPTAT usage, where there were nearly 36.5 million pageviews. We note three general kinds of usage patterns: minimalists, traditionalists, and dabblers.

Introduction

The original tutorial and test on *How to Recognize Plagiarism* was developed for use by students in the Instructional Systems Technology (IST) department at Indiana University, first released in September 2002. The first author had led a student team in his advanced production course earlier that year to design and develop the original version, now referred to as the legacy version: https://plagiarism.iu.edu/credits.html.

Other instructors and students soon discovered these online resources on the Web. Although mostly at Indiana University at first, instructors from other universities and even secondary school teachers started to adopt the original tutorial and test. Web traffic from outside Indiana University quickly surpassed use on our IU campuses, including visitors from other countries.

By word of mouth, and through web search results, the online tutorial and test usage has been increasing each year—with more than 125 million total pageviews since its launch (see Figures 3.1 and 3.2).

The plagiarism tutorial design team has consisted of a variety of members during the first 17+ years of design, development, modification, and

DOI: 10.4324/9781003176343-03

Figure 3.1 Home Page of the Original Tutorial, circa 2003

usability testing. We refer to the changing group as the plagiarism tutorial *design team* (see https://plagiarism.iu.edu/acknowledge.html).

The design team has learned through correspondence initiated by instructors that many now require their students to take this test. We have no control over who uses our tests and for what purposes. Our goal is to help people understand what plagiarism is, so that they do not commit plagiarism in their writing and presentations. At this time, anyone is welcome to use our learning resources and tests for free.

Numerous improvements have been made to IPTAT over the years Indiana University Plagiarism Tutorials and Tests (2002–2020). A summary of the first 14 years is described by Frick et al. (2018). For a history of changes from 2013 through the present, see: https://plagiarism.iu.edu/recentChanges.html. Starting in 2013 we made significant changes to the Certification Test in response to instructors informing us that students had discovered ways to cheat, and even pointed out answer keys posted on the Web. Details of changes in Certification Testing are reported by Frick et al. (2018). Bottom line: we made it much harder to cheat by creating large

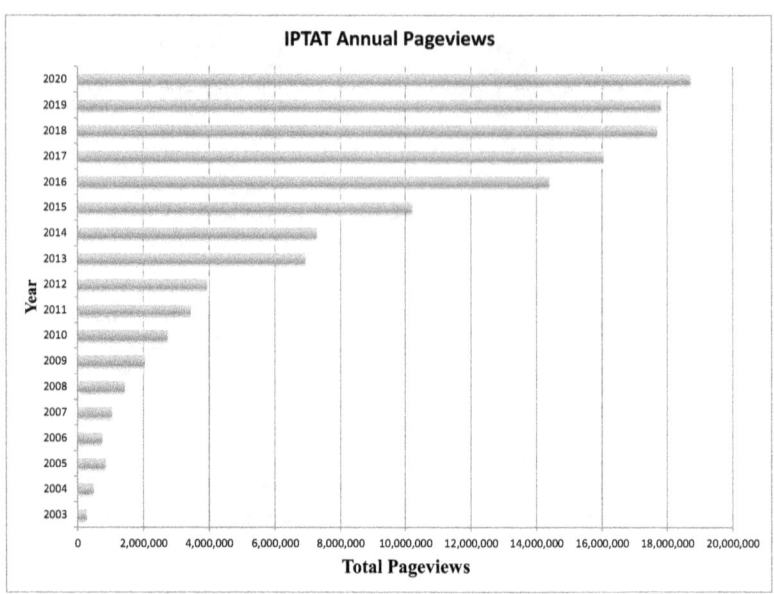

Figure 3.2 Annual Pageviews of the Indiana University Plagiarism Tutorial and Tests (IPTAT), from 2003 through 2020.

test item pools and selecting 10 questions at random for each Certification Test. There are trillions of combinations of 10-item tests (see explanation at https://plagiarism.iu.edu/faq.html#faq2). Our reasoning was to make it easier to learn to recognize plagiarism than to cheat on the Certification Test.

Major Redesign of IPTAT in 2015

The design team redesigned the IPTAT for several reasons: First and foremost, the design team wanted to improve the effectiveness of the tutorial. The new design implemented First Principles of Instruction (Merrill, 2002, 2013, 2020). Merrill (2002) had claimed that—regardless of specific content, teaching methods, or programmatic subject matter—student learning would be promoted to the extent that each of the First Principles is implemented in design of instruction. In addition to using First Principles, the design team wanted to carry out research to evaluate how these five principles of instruction affect student learning (Frick & Dagli, 2016). In particular, is Merrill's claim supported by empirical evidence on student usage of parts of the IPTAT and successful learning as indicated by passing a Certification Test?

First Principles include:

1. *Provision of authentic tasks or problems*, sequenced from simple to complex,
2. *Activation* to help students connect what they already know with what is to be newly learned,
3. *Demonstration* of what is to be learned,
4. *Application*, where students try to do the tasks or solve problems with instructor guidance and feedback, and
5. *Integration* of what is learned into students' own lives.

A variety of pedagogical methods can be used to implement each principle, depending on the types of learning objectives, content being taught, and levels of schooling (elementary, secondary, postsecondary). See Merrill (2013, 2020) for an in-depth description and numerous examples of First Principles of Instruction.

The redesign process took place over a period of about nine months, with the bulk of the development and production completed in late 2015. The new design went live on January 2, 2016. The new design and homepage are illustrated in Figure 3.3.

Authentic Problems Principle

This principle required us to design a series of authentic problems in recognizing plagiarism, arranged from simple to complex. We did so, as indicated on the menu at: https://plagiarism.iu.edu/tutorials/index.html.

As can be seen in Figure 3.4, problems are arranged at five levels of difficulty in recognizing plagiarism: basic, novice, intermediate, advanced, and expert. At each level of difficulty, we provide activation, demonstration, application, integration, and a practice test.

Activation Principle

We decided to design and develop ten video cases as a means of student activation—providing real-world cases for students to experience vicariously. Storytelling is an instructional method which we implemented in our new design to embody the *activation* principle (e.g., see Andrews et al., 2009). View an example of a video case at: https://plagiarism.iu.edu/tutorials/task4/activation.html. Similar video cases that tell stories are provided at each of the five levels of task difficulty (see Figure 3.5).

32   *The IU Plagiarism Tutorials and Tests*

**How to Recognize Plagiarism:
Tutorials and Tests**

Welcome to the Indiana University Plagiarism Tutorials and Tests

Learn how to recognize plagiarism, test your understanding, and earn a certificate.

To begin, watch this brief video of a teacher meeting with a student who has committed plagiarism. Click on the one-minute video below.

Video too slow? Click here for lower quality video.

Why is it important to avoid plagiarism?

The academic community highly values the acknowledgment of contributions to knowledge. When you properly acknowledge the contributions to knowledge made by other people, you are showing respect for their work. You are giving credit where credit is due. You are not misleading the reader to believe that your ideas and words are solely your own.

The disciplinary consequences of documented plagiarism at Indiana University (IU) can be severe. As a student you could receive a failing grade or be expelled from the university. In extreme cases, your degree could be revoked if plagiarism is discovered after you have graduated.

Thus, avoiding plagiarism is important -- both in writing and speaking. This instruction will help you to understand and recognize plagiarism.

How much time does it take to learn from tutorials and to take tests?

Expect to spend about 2 hours learning from this instruction and taking Certification Tests. Successful students typically divide their learning into 3 sessions of about 35 to 40 minutes each, viewing an average of 77 pages altogether. Completing a Certification Test usually takes 5 to 10 minutes. If you do not pass, feedback is provided about the kinds of mistakes you made. You can take as many Certification Tests as you want.

Click the link below to continue.

Next Page: Organization of this Instruction

Start Here: Welcome

Read Overview

Learn through Tutorials

Register for Certification Tests

Take Certification Tests

Retrieve and Validate Certificates

See FAQs

View Resources

View Site Map

Acknowledge Site

Figure 3.3   Screenshot of IPTAT "Welcome" Page in 2020

The IU Plagiarism Tutorials and Tests 33

Basic Level: Recognize the basic difference between:
- *avoiding* plagiarism, and
- *committing* plagiarism.

Novice Level: When *one source is used*, recognize a proper quotation from an improper quotation:
- a *proper quotation* of someone else's words, and
- provision of the appropriate citation and reference.

Intermediate Level: When *one source is used*, recognize a proper paraphrase from an improper paraphrase:
- a *proper paraphrase* of someone else's words, and
- provision of the appropriate citation and reference.

Advanced Level: When *one source is used*, recognize various combinations of:
- *proper/improper paraphrasing*, and
- *proper/improper quotations*.

Expert Level: Put it all together. When *two or more sources are used*, recognize various combinations of:
- *proper/improper paraphrasing*, and
- *proper/improper quotations*.

Register for Certification Tests

Take Certification Tests

Retrieve and Validate Certificates

See FAQs

View Resources

View Site Map

Acknowledge Site

Figure 3.4 Five Levels of Difficulty in Recognizing Plagiarism

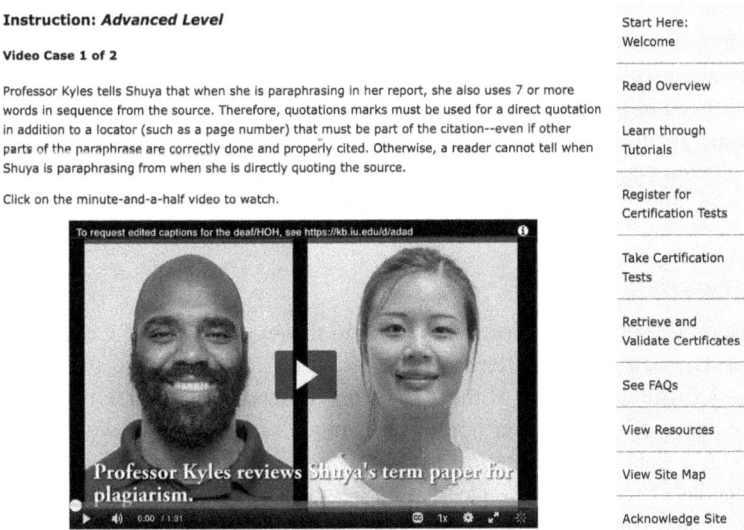

Figure 3.5 Example of the Activation Principle for Advanced Level of Problem Difficulty

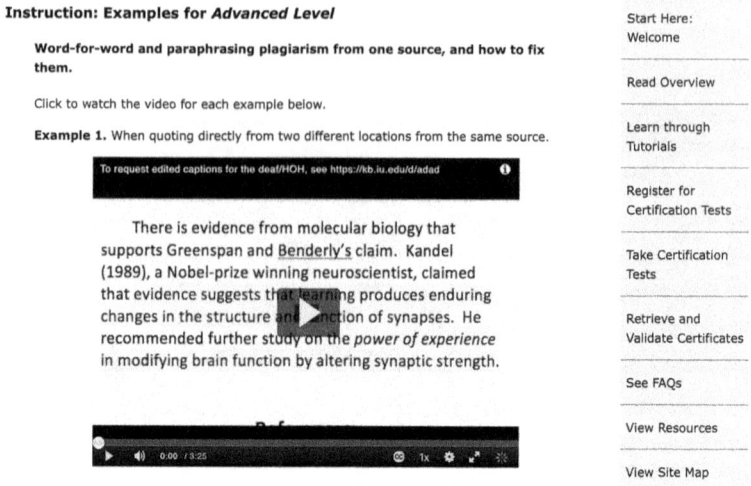

Figure 3.6 One of 12 Screencasts that Illustrate Plagiarism and How to Fix It, for the Demonstration Principle

Demonstration Principle

Here we chose to design 12 screencasts that dynamically portray the writing of a whole, short paper (overlaid with audio explanation of ongoing visual changes in the paper and why they were being made). Examples dynamically show the author committing plagiarism and how he fixes it in order to avoid plagiarism. See, for example, demonstrations at the advanced task level: https://plagiarism.iu.edu/tutorials/task4/demonstration.html.

Application Principle

Here we developed questions similar to those on the IPTAT Certification Tests, but with two differences. Question difficulty matches the level of task difficulty at each of the five levels. Immediate feedback on the correctness of each answer is provided. In addition, if the answer is incorrect, a detailed explanation of why it is incorrect is provided. Also, if needed, explanation is provided on how to correctly fix the student version to avoid plagiarism. For example, see the advanced level practice items: https://plagiarism.iu.edu/practiceTest.php?task=4&item=1 (see Figures 3.7 and 3.8).

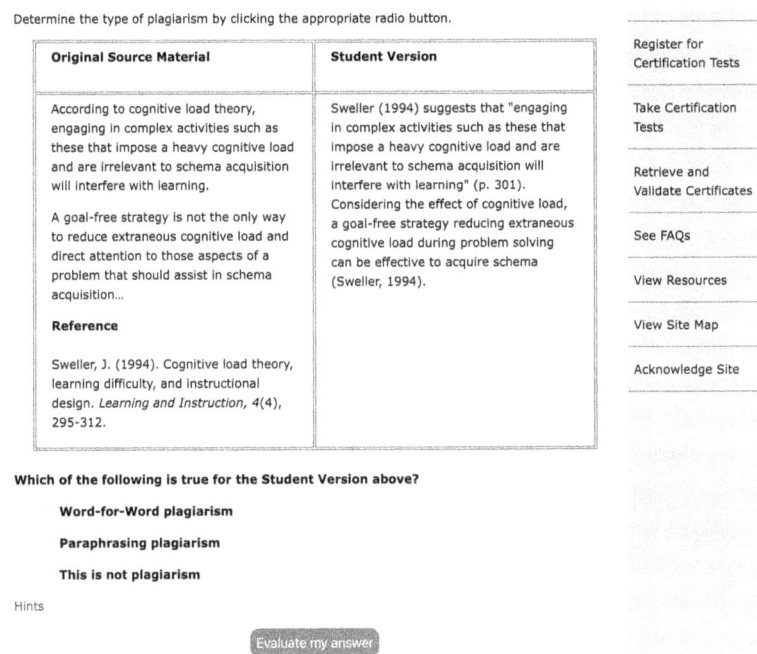

Figure 3.7 Example of the Application Principle at the Advanced Level of Problem Difficulty

Integration Principle

This was perhaps the most challenging principle of instruction to implement in an online tutorial with no human instructor regularly available. We decided to do this by giving students an opportunity to reflect on what they just learned and how it might be used in their own lives. See for example the integration activity at the advanced level of difficulty: https://plagiarism.iu.edu/tutorials/task4/integration.html. Here we do not provide feedback on what students write in the text input box, but we do store their comments for later qualitative content analysis to be done as part of research studies (see Figure 3.9).

Certification Tests

We have designed the Certification Tests (CT) so that there are literally trillions of unique tests. After registering and logging in to take a CT, a student will get only one attempt at each test taken. Students can take as

Figure 3.8

Question 1 answer is incorrect. Please see the feedback below.

Original Source Material:	Student Version:
According to cognitive load theory, engaging in complex activities such as these that impose a heavy cognitive load and are irrelevant to schema acquisition will interfere with learning.	Sweller (1994) suggests that "engaging in complex activities such as these that impose a heavy cognitive load and are irrelevant to schema acquisition will interfere with learning" (p. 301). Considering the effect of cognitive load, a goal-free strategy reducing extraneous cognitive load during problem solving can be effective to acquire schema (Sweller, 1994).
A goal-free strategy is not the only way to reduce extraneous cognitive load and direct attention to those aspects of a problem that should assist in schema acquisition...	
Reference	
Sweller, J. (1994). Cognitive load theory, learning difficulty, and instructional design. *Learning and Instruction, 4*(4), 295-312.	

Explanation:	Correct Version:
The student version is both **word-for-word and paraphrasing plagiarism**. Even though the student provided quotation marks around the ideas of the author, and full in-text citation with the author, date, and locator in the body of the paper, he or she did not use the full bibliographic reference.	Sweller (1994) suggests that "engaging in complex activities such as these that impose a heavy cognitive load and are irrelevant to schema acquisition will interfere with learning" (p. 301). Considering the effect of cognitive load, a goal-free strategy reducing extraneous cognitive load during problem solving can be effective to acquire schema (Sweller, 1994).
Although the student has paraphrased the ideas of the author and included full in-text citation with the author and date, no reference is provided.	**Reference**
Note: If the student version contains BOTH word-for-word and paraphrasing plagiarism, you should select **word-for-word**.	Sweller, J. (1994). Cognitive load theory, learning difficulty, and instructional design. *Learning and Instruction, 4*(4), 295-312.

Read Overview

Learn through Tutorials

Register for Certification Tests

Take Certification Tests

Retrieve and Validate Certificates

See FAQs

View Resources

View Site Map

Acknowledge Site

Please also see the item pattern for Question 1: Delinked Dupe.

Figure 3.8 Example of Feedback to an Incorrect Answer for the Application Principle at the Advanced Level of Difficulty

many tests as they want, but there is a 40-minute time limit on each test (see Figures 3.10 through 3.13).

There is a large pool of test items for undergraduate and advanced high school students, and an even larger and more difficult item pool for masters and doctoral students. Ten items are selected at random from the appropriate pool for each test, resulting in trillions of combinations of unique ten-item CTs.

Feedback on a CT is adaptive and depends on how well a student performs. If a student fails a test (see example in Figure 3.12), then the test feedback page provides additional information on the kinds of mistakes made. For

The IU Plagiarism Tutorials and Tests 37

**How to Recognize Plagiarism:
Tutorials and Tests**

Instruction: Reflect on what you've learned at the *Advanced Level*

You should avoid both *word-for-word* and *paraphrasing* plagiarism. Think about a situation in your own life where you would want to write or speak about *someone else's ideas*, where you would want to both directly quote and summarize their ideas.

Click in the text box below, and briefly tell us about this. We will not share your comments with others.

[Continue to Practice Test at the Advanced Level]

Start Here:
Welcome

Read Overview

Learn through Tutorials

Register for Certification Tests

Take Certification Tests

Figure 3.9 Example of a Reflection Activity, for the Integration Principle at the Advanced Level of Problem Difficulty

Take Certification Tests

Each randomly selected question on a test provides source material from another author and a sample of student writing. You must determine whether the student version is word-for-word plagiarism, paraphrasing plagiarism, or not plagiarism. The tests are challenging for most people, requiring concentration and attention to detail.

To pass a Certification Test, you must answer at least 9 out of 10 questions correctly within 40 minutes. Why? If you pass, your Certificate will be e-mailed to you, and you can view your Certificate online. Very important, you *and your instructor* can retrieve and validate it later to ensure it is not counterfeit.

If you do not pass a Certification Test, you *will* receive feedback on *specific kinds of mistakes* you are making. Click on the links provided in the test feedback to see examples of the kinds of questions you missed, and why you missed them.

You can take more tests, but each test is different. Some questions may look the same as ones you saw before, but differ in small *but important details* which affect which answer is correct. See this support tool for additional help.

We do *not* tell you which questions you answered incorrectly on a Certification Test.

Why? Because it makes it harder to create answer keys for cheating, as was widely occuring in the past. It's not because we can't provide correct answers, or don't understand the importance of feedback in the learning process. The Certification Tests are designed for *valid assessment* of your ability to classify types of plagiarism, *not* designed as instruments for learning *per se*. That's what the tutorials are for, which include practice questions with explanatory feedback on how to correct your mistakes.

Click a button below to login for a test:

What age group do you belong to?

[I'm an undergraduate college student or advanced high school student]

[I'm a master's or doctoral student in graduate school]

Register for Certification Tests

Take Certification Tests

Retrieve and Validate Certificates

See FAQs

View Resources

View Site Map

Acknowledge Site

Figure 3.10 Example of the IPTAT Certification Test Starting Page

The IU Plagiarism Tutorials and Tests

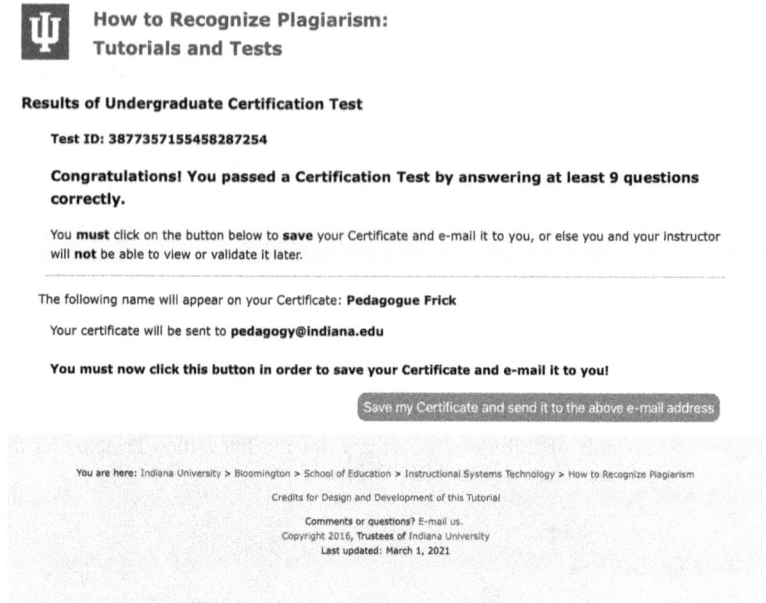

Figure 3.11 Example of Certification Test Feedback when Passing

example, in Figure 3.12, the student made one kind of mistake. Students can then click on links to each type of mistake (referred to as patterns of plagiarism at https://plagiarism.iu.edu/plagiarismPatterns/index.html).

If a student passes a CT, they can get the Certificate e-mailed to the address at which they registered. Certificates can be retrieved later by a student via logging in. Instructors can validate each Certificate by entering the unique Test ID and either the IP number or the e-mail address associated with that student's test. Instructors like this feature, since it discourages students from submitting forged or counterfeit Certificates.

Certification Tests are difficult for most students, and the graduate level tests are harder than the ones for undergraduates and advanced high school students. Since the new design went live in 2016, about one out of seven tests attempted is passed.

Summary of Changes to the Newly Designed IPTAT in 2015

- Instruction is now organized by levels of difficulty (basic, novice, intermediate, advanced, and expert).
- Students can view ten video cases which illustrate consequences of student plagiarism, as students interact with their instructors or peers.

The IU Plagiarism Tutorials and Tests 39

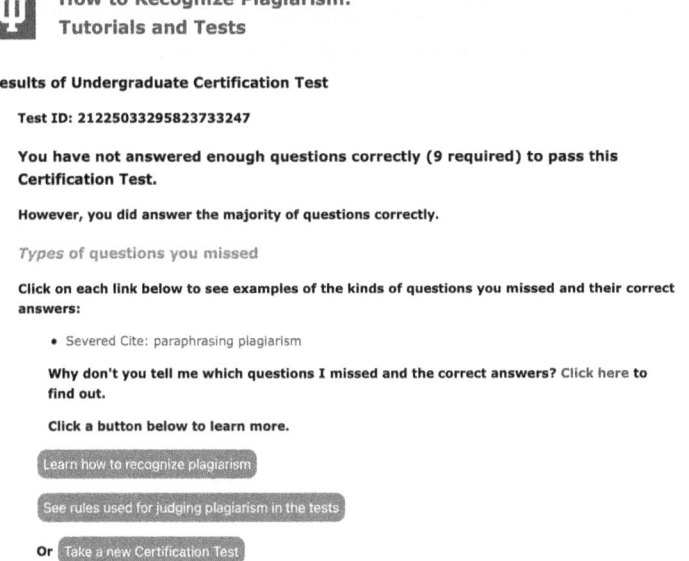

Figure 3.12 Example of Certification Test Feedback when Not Passing

- Students can view 12 dynamic screencasts of examples that show plagiarism while a scholarly paper is being written, and what to do to fix the problems.
- Students can reflect on how they might use what they have been learning.
- Students can take practice tests at each level of difficulty, with detailed feedback on questions missed.
- Certification Test item inventories have been greatly expanded.
- Certificates earned for passing a test in 2016 or later can be retrieved, validated, and e-mailed by both students *and their instructors*.
- The web page layout is easier to use on devices with smaller displays (smartphones and tablets).

What's the Same?

- The goal has not been changed. We still expect students to learn to recognize the difference between plagiarism (word-for-word and paraphrasing) and non-plagiarism.
- The online tutorial and tests are still freely available to anyone and can be used for any non-profit educational purpose.
- Students are required to register and login before they can take a test.

- Test questions are randomly selected from very large inventories of items each time students take a test.
- Patterns of plagiarism remained unchanged, used primarily for illustrating types of errors made if students do not pass a test.

Usage of IPTAT from 2019 and 2020

As can be seen in Figure 3.14, there were nearly 36.5 million pageviews in this two-year interval. Notable are the peak usage periods. These spikes are associated with beginnings of semesters or terms in K-12 schools and universities. Each August/September and each January/February cycle shows this pattern. The bottoms of spikes are typically Saturdays of each week,

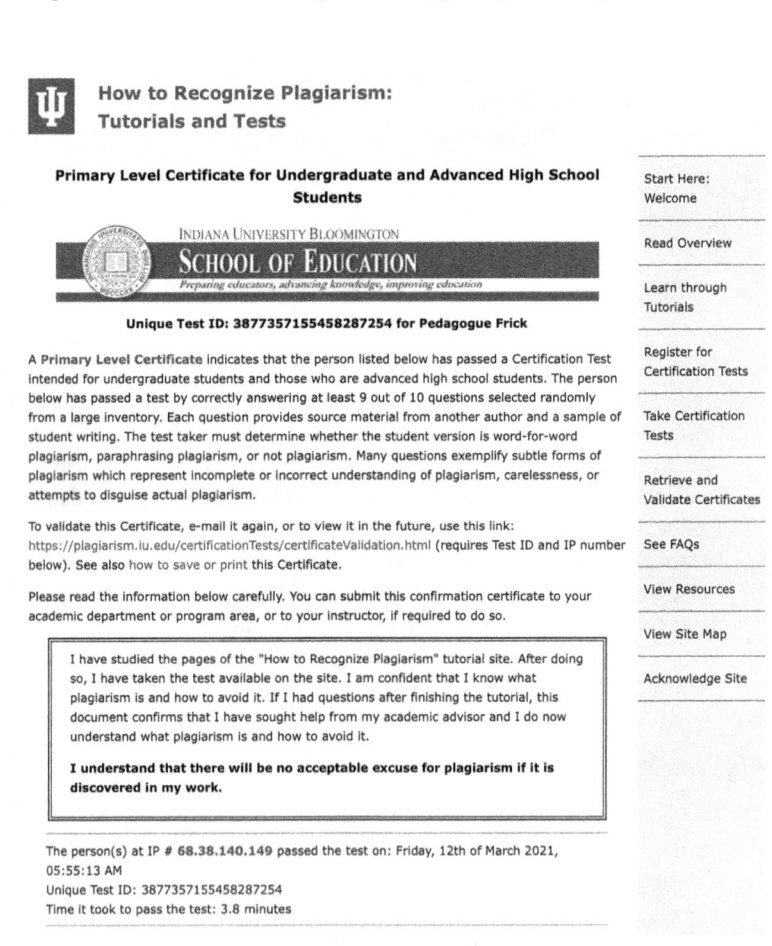

Figure 3.13 Example of a Primary Level Certificate when Passing

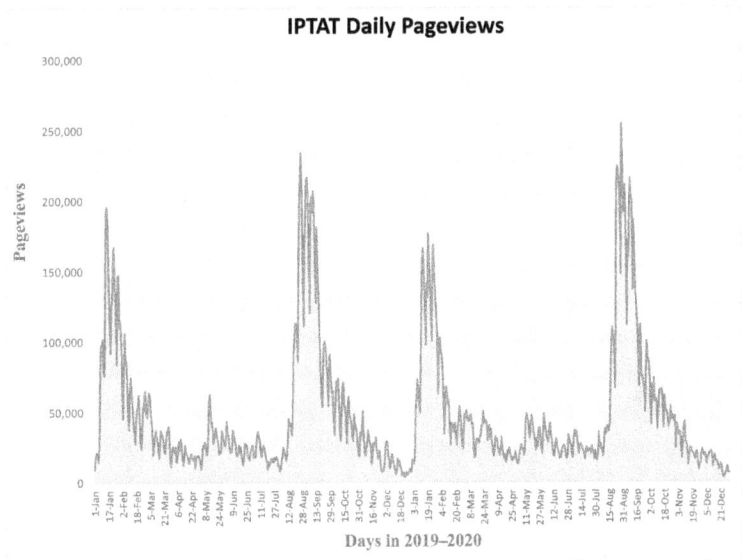

Figure 3.14 Daily IPTAT Pageviews from Google Analytics between January 1, 2019 and December 31, 2020 (total of 36,485,235 pageviews)

when usage normally drops off dramatically when compared with usage from Sundays through Fridays.

Google Analytics (GA) reports over 918,000 visitors to IPTAT. The counting of visitors is complicated by the fact that many users switch devices from one GA session to the next, each of which has a unique digital device fingerprint, and by the fact that many users never register to take a Certification Test. This is explained in more detail in Chapter 4.

We know from observing GA 'behavior flows' that there are three primary user strategies:

- Minimalists
- Traditionalists
- Dabblers

Minimalists

One group goes straight to the Certification Tests, since they apparently want to get a Certificate with the least amount of time and effort required. They register right away, login, and then start taking tests. As illustrated in Map 2.1 in Chapter 2, Sam is typical of a Minimalist. Although not shown in Chapter 2, Sam returned to IPTAT at a later time, took more tests, used only parts of IPTAT to understand and correct his mistakes, and continued until he passed a CT. This is a typical pattern for Minimalists.

Traditionalists

The other major group largely follows the instruction as we designed it, usually by clicking on the "next page" links, until they are ready to take a Certification Test. As we illustrated in Chapter 2, Melinda is typical of a Traditionalist. These students usually do *not* register until they want to start taking CTs. Traditionalists typically require fewer attempts to pass a CT when compared to the Minimalists. Melinda was exceptional, as illustrated in Chapter 2, by passing a CT on her first try. Most traditionalists require multiple attempts before they pass.

Dabblers

We know less about these users, since they do not register to take a Certification Test, at least not on their current devices. They do not stay on the IPTAT website very long, about 10 minutes on average. We call this group Dabblers, due to the relatively high GA bounce rate reported (no interaction with a page and then they leave the IPTAT site).

On the other hand, Minimalists and Traditionalists often spend two hours or more until they pass a CT. A very high percentage of these users report when registering that they are using IPTAT because it is an assignment or requirement by their instructor or school.

Registrants

We do keep our own records of students who register with our IPTAT. From our MySQL database at Indiana University, we have records of 381,724 users who successfully registered by going to their e-mail and clicking on a link to confirm their registration between January 1, 2019 and December 31, 2020. We have further records that indicate 315,376 passed at least one Certification Test during that interval. Some of these Certificants ($n = 8,828$) had registered prior to 2019 but passed a CT during the 2019–2020 interval. Furthermore, there were registrants in 2019 and 2020 who had not passed a CT ($n = 75,065$). Thus, the total number registrants was 390,654 (315,376 + 75,065), and the proportion who had passed a CT was 0.81 (315,376/390,654).

Even more important is that we have found, as described in Chapters 2 and 4, that successful students (i.e., who pass a CT) on average are between three and four times more likely per learning journey to select IPTAT web pages which were designed using First Principles of Instruction when compared with unsuccessful students. We also have found that students who do *not* complete any of the tutorials and practice tests are between 90 and 95 percent likely to fail their first Certification Test. Students who *do* complete at least some of the tutorials often need to take more than one test until they pass.

User-Developer Feedback Loop

Nearly every IPTAT page has a link in the footer so that users can send e-mail to us with comments and questions. This is an important feedback loop that has helped us to improve the design, based on what students and instructors tell us.

In order to reduce the number of e-mail replies needed, we developed a frequently asked questions (FAQ) page in 2018: https://plagiarism.iu.edu/faq.html. The FAQ page has greatly reduced the amount of e-mail we receive, now typically four to six per week, though higher during peak usage times (see Figure 3.14) and lower during other non-peak times (e.g., summers and later in semesters).

The most frequent question or complaint typically comes from *Minimalist* users. They are frustrated because they have not been able to pass a Certification Test thus far, and they complain that the tests are so "hard". They further ask, "Why don't you tell me the correct answers or at least which questions I missed?" Many of these students believe that if they just keep trying to take a test (without doing any of our IPTAT instruction), they will eventually pass. Unfortunately, their belief is often mistaken. They cannot pass a test just by guessing or trying to game the system. It is also difficult to cheat using answer keys, because there are so many questions in our item pools; about a third of them look the same but differ in subtle details that affect which answer is correct; and none of the same questions are likely to be repeated from one test to the next. These student questions and complaints are addressed in FAQs: https://plagiarism.iu.edu/faq.html#faq2. We tell them up-front on the IPTAT page for starting a test that they are more likely to pass if they take advantage of the instruction and practice with feedback in the tutorials: https://plagiarism.iu.edu/certificationTests/index.html.

We rarely get complaints from *Traditionalist* users, and when we do, they are "sure" that the testing system is broken, when in fact it is working as it was designed. Usually, these users are missing some important detail for classifying types of plagiarism. We have recently added a further FAQ for this situation: https://plagiarism.iu.edu/faq.html#faq16. In early 2020, we also added an interactive decision support for test takers: https://plagiarism.iu.edu/decide/.

In summary, this user-developer feedback loop has been mutually beneficial. It helps us improve the IPTAT over time, as well as to address specific user concerns. In the past several years, maintenance of IPTAT has taken only a few hours per week. Otherwise, the IPTAT keeps running; students keep learning; and most pass a Certification Test.

We use Google Analytics regularly to see what is going on with the IPTAT website. The GA Realtime tool further provides insights for how many users are on the system at any point in time, where they are located, and what pages they are viewing. We also monitor usage by examining our IU MySQL records and our Certification Test logs.

What About COVID?

During the last three quarters of 2020, COVID impacted many people's lives worldwide, and many teachers and students were forced into remote teaching and learning for the first time, with little notice and preparation (e.g., see Frick, 2020). Just before submitting this book manuscript to the publisher, an experienced instructional designer and college instructor who reviewed it asked: "Did we see anything different in IPTAT usage during the second year of the Big Study?"

The short answer: no. The kinds of usage patterns of IPTAT in 2020 were very stable, as they have been since 2016 after we had redesigned it with First Principles of Instruction. As Figure 3.14 shows, the peak usage at beginnings of semesters continued in August and September 2020, and the patterns in the first five quarters appeared to be no different in the last three quarters of the Big Study. And as Figure 3.2 indicates, the overall usage of IPTAT continued to increase in 2020 when compared with previous years. But that has been the trend since 2002.

If anything, the only notable difference was the balance of unsolicited comments from students and teachers that were shared with us as part of the important user-developer feedback loop described above. Although we have not done a thorough analysis of those comments, there appear to have been fewer complaints by frustrated students and more "thank-you" comments sent to us. However, we should not draw any conclusions, since the number of these comments is quite small, typically one or two per week. As mentioned above, our FAQ page addresses and answers the most common questions we have received in the past. That FAQ page has consistently ranked in the top 15 IPTAT pages viewed since we first added it, prior to the Big Study.

We especially note the remarkable consistency of IPTAT usage patterns since 2016. The main reason we did not report all five years of usage in the Big Study here was that the findings from the first three years were very similar, telling us nothing new. The nearly 1.87 million temporal maps in the Big Study revealed the same patterns consistently, quarter by quarter. While IPTAT pageviews typically peak at the beginnings of semesters, the patterns we report here have been very stable.

Next, in Chapter 4, we explain in more detail how we carried out the Big Study in 2019 and 2020.

References

Andrews, D. H., Hull, T. D., & Donahue, J. A. (2009). Storytelling as an instructional method: Descriptions and research questions. *The Interdisciplinary Journal of Problem-Based Learning*, *3*(2). http://dx.doi.org/10.7771/1541-5015.1063

Frick, T. W. (2020). Education systems and technology in 1990, 2020, and beyond. *TechTrends*. https://doi.org/10.1007/s11528-020-00527-y

Frick, T. W., & Dagli, C. (2016). MOOCs for research: The case of the Indiana University plagiarism tutorials and tests. *Technology, Knowledge and Learning*, *21*(2), 255–276.

Frick, T. W., Dagli, C., Kwon, K., & Tomita, K. (2018). Indiana University plagiarism tutorials and tests: 14 Years of worldwide learning online. In B. Hokanson et al. (Eds.), *Educational technology and narrative: Story and instructional design* (Chapter 16, pp. 191–205). Springer.

Indiana University Plagiarism Tutorials and Tests. (2002–2020). How to recognize plagiarism. https://plagiarism.iu.edu

Merrill, M. D. (2002). First principles of instruction. *Educational Technology Research & Development*, *50*(3), 43–59.

Merrill, M. D. (2013). *First principles of instruction: Identifying and designing effective, efficient, and engaging instruction*. Pfeiffer.

Merrill, M. D. (2020). *M. David Merrill's first principles of instruction*. Association for Educational Communications and Technology.

4 More Details of the Big Study

Summary: We report on our Big Study in greater detail, which was previewed in the second chapter. We demonstrate how we arrived at our findings over a two-year interval, by illustrating APT for one quarter, and then we describe how we combined quarters using a spreadsheet. The Big Study involved students from 213 countries and territories worldwide, mostly between 14 and 44 years old. We describe how Google Analytics was used to track IPTAT usage. Then we illustrate how segmenting of temporal maps and logical conditions were applied via Google Analytics in order to carry out parts of APT queries. We further illustrate how we used a spreadsheet with cell formulas to complete the APT calculations. We provide further details on how Google Analytics identifies users. We conclude by summarizing demographic characteristics of students who registered to take IPTAT Certification Tests.

Discovery of Google Analytics for Doing APT

We did not plan for the Big Study to happen this way. After redesigning and implementing the Indiana University Plagiarism Tutorials and Tests (IPTAT), our original plan for Analysis of Patterns in Time (APT) Study 2 was outlined in Frick and Dagli (2016, p. 257):

> Behind the scenes, IPTAT software will create individual temporal maps that track each student's choices as he or she navigates and completes learning activities in the IPTAT, including that student's performance on a Certification Test.

But the Big Study reported here has not happened this way, technically speaking. We got lucky due to serendipity when the first author discovered a way to approximate APT by leveraging Google Analytics (GA) reporting tools as an initial step in early 2020. Then he subsequently invented step-by-step Excel spreadsheet formulas to turn results from GA reports into the APT results we needed for evaluating the effectiveness of First Principles of Instruction (FPI).

DOI: 10.4324/9781003176343-04

More Details of the Big Study   47

A bit of history here will help explain what has happened so far.

As we were in the process of planning the newer version of IPTAT in 2015, we had decided to continue our own data collection scheme (see Frick & Dagli, 2016, p. 268). First, we decided that students need not register in IPTAT until and unless they want to take a Certification Test. This would allow users to do the tutorials anonymously and learn to recognize plagiarism without registering. It also would reduce the burden on IU web servers, since most of IPTAT can be accessed through normal requests for HTML files. PHP scripts for creating dynamic web pages require more processing time for web server delivery. PHP-generated pages are unnecessary for accessing most of the IPTAT website. We were already aware of very heavy usage of the IPTAT website at the beginnings of semesters. See Chapter 3 for a description of exponential growth in IPTAT usage, especially Figure 3.2 and the bi-annual usage peaks in Figure 3.14.

We added GA into the mix in late 2015, almost as an afterthought. Indiana University Information Technology Services (UITS) had discontinued provision of server statistics to IU web developers and recommended GA as one of several alternatives.

When setting up a website with Google Analytics, GA provides a snippet of JavaScript for customizing website tracking of user interactions. For example, the current code in most of our IPTAT web pages is:

```
<script async src="https://www.googletagmanager.com/gtag/js?id=
    UA-71928711-1"></script>
<script>
window.dataLayer = window.dataLayer || [];
function gtag(){dataLayer.push(arguments);}
gtag('js', new Date());
gtag('config', 'UA-71928711-1');
</script>
```

Readers should further note that GA is a software product that is likely to evolve over time. For example, in mid-October 2020, Google introduced a newer method referred to as Google Analytics 4 (GA4). The previous method has been referred to as Universal Analytics (UA), which is what IPTAT has utilized since 2016. Later in this chapter we discuss differences between UA and GA4, and also provide a further APT example with GA4.

We did not know in 2015 that Google software engineers had already implemented a way to create temporal maps for Analysis of Patterns in Time. It is a happy coincidence that we discovered this fact nearly five years after the redesign of IPTAT. Google Analytics was developed primarily for a different purpose, but we have a common goal: *to predict outcomes based on earlier patterns observed in temporal maps*. Google's business clients are interested in temporal patterns which predict sales of their clients' services and products.

48 More Details of the Big Study

On the other hand, in the Big Study here, we are interested in temporal patterns which predict subsequent learning achievement outcomes—in particular, patterns that indicate effectiveness of First Principles of Instruction.

How did we do this? This chapter explains in detail what we have done and how.

Important Concepts for Doing Analysis of Patterns in Time

As discussed in Chapter 1 and illustrated by the Oregon Trail metaphor, *temporal maps* are the main data source for doing APT. In Chapter 2, we provided two examples of specific temporal maps: Sam's and Melinda's learning journeys. In their most basic form, temporal maps are special kinds of tables: rows which are identified by successive date/time notations, and columns which characterize specific events that occurred at each particular time. Without such maps, we could not do APT as Frick (1983, 1990) envisioned it.

In addition to having temporal maps as data sources, the second big concept is segmenting temporal event occurrences by APT queries. APT queries are ways of *segmenting* events within temporal maps into chunks that match the query elements. Frick (1983, 1990) referred to APT query *phrases* that consisted of *phrase segments*, and GA currently refers to *segmenting* as a basic way of classifying temporal maps and contents within maps. But these are essentially the same idea, just different terminology. GA does not refer to APT *per se*, but has made it possible to do some kinds of APT nonetheless. APT was invented in the 1970s. GA effectively started in 2006, after buying a company that had created software for measuring temporal maps (Adaptive Path). See https://en.wikipedia.org/wiki/Google_Analytics#History.

Thus, these are two very big ideas: *temporal maps* and *segmenting*. The contents of temporal maps and ways of segmenting such maps depend on the particular purpose of the research and evaluation that is being done. Are we trying to predict future events, given a starting point? Or are we trying to retrodict earlier temporal events, given an endpoint?

Two Fundamental Ways of Temporal Segmenting: Prediction and Retrodiction

In prediction, we want to know that when such and such is the case, what is likely to follow at a *later* time? In retrodiction, we want to know that when such and such is the case, what was likely to have occurred at an *earlier* time?

As an example of prediction, if it is the case that nimbus stratus clouds are present and the outside air temperature is below 32 degrees Fahrenheit, and the barometric pressure is less than 30 pounds per square inch, what is the likelihood that it will snow at a later time?

More Details of the Big Study 49

As an example of retrodiction, and the focus of our Big Study here, when students pass a Certification Test, what is the likelihood that they experienced First Principles of Instruction at an earlier time? And, when they have not passed a Certification Test, what is the likelihood that they experienced First Principles of Instruction?

Our significant breakthrough for the Big Study was the discovery of ways to define GA segments. Tools for defining segments were found in UA administrative settings under ways of creating personal views of IPTAT website data, separated from the main analytic tools for Realtime, Audience, Acquisition, Behavior, and Conversions. It is noteworthy that in GA4 making comparisons and defining segments for comparisons are now more prominent in most of their main analytic tools—in order to do comparisons of subsets of audiences and event conditions in GA4 reports.

The other significant breakthrough was when the first author discovered ways of doing further segmenting in reports of IPTAT user behaviors, that is, in classifying what web pages they viewed. He realized that if we segmented learning journeys according to whether they were successful or not (whether or not a Certification Test had been passed), then we could further segment those subgroups according to types of pages viewed *within* their respective temporal maps. *This would allow us to do retrodictive APT queries about student experiences of First Principles of Instruction!*

So just how did we do this?

Temporal Segmenting by Quarters One at a Time

Once the basic strategy for implementing retrodictive APT queries was identified, the next discoveries involved limitations and assumptions in GA tracking and reporting methods. The major limitation we identified was that segments of tracking data were limited to 90 days at a time in GA reports—in effect to intervals no longer than a quarter of a year. We decided that we would look at temporal data on IPTAT usage in 2019 and 2020, that is, during eight quarters. Once we had GA results for each quarter, then we pasted those numbers into an Excel spreadsheet, with one worksheet for each quarter, and then created a summary worksheet that combined the results from the quarterly worksheets. We have already reported results of the summary worksheet in Chapter 2, Tables 2.2 and 2.3.

Thus, we used an additional software tool, Microsoft Excel, in order to complete our APT analyses. We could have used a different spreadsheet tool. The main point here is that we used available software tools to facilitate APT, much as we have done historically. This process was consistently driven by the overall big concepts of (1) temporal maps, and (2) ways to segment these maps temporally.

Here's what we did in the Big Study.

Retrodictive APT Queries

Endpoint Condition Defined

The basic segment types we wanted to create were successful and unsuccessful learning journeys. This was done by using the Google Analytics UA website tool at https://analytics.google.com/ and signing into the Analytics Account that we created earlier for the IPTAT website. Then we selected Administrative settings and the UA View for Segments (under Personal Tools and Assets). We defined a segment for "Users Who Passed" and a segment for "Users Who Have Not Passed" as follows:

Users Who Passed

This segment was defined by creating a condition that was defined by filtering users to *include* those who have visited an IPTAT web page filename that contains '/mail'. There are only two IPTAT web pages that will match that condition: '/mailCertificateUG.php' and '/mailCertificateGR.php'. The only way a user can view either of these pages is, after registering for IPTAT, they login and take *and pass* a Certification Test. Then, on the results page, they click on a button to save and mail their Certificate. This button then links to one of these two web page files, depending on whether an Undergraduate and Advanced High School Certification Test was passed or whether it was a Graduate level test, respectively (see Chapter 3, Figure 3.11).

Users Who Have Not Passed

This segment was defined by creating a condition by filtering users who remain after *excluding* those who have visited a web page filename that contains '/mail'. This segment definition thus identifies a subgroup of users who have not passed an IPTAT Certification Test.

In effect, these two segments have defined mutually exclusive and exhaustive subsets of IPTAT user learning journeys.

Apply the Endpoint Condition to the GA Audience Reporting Tool (UA)

The next step involved the creation of a GA Audience report. When segments are used to create subsets in GA, we were limited to 90 days at a time. We illustrate this here for Quarter 1, 2020. Then we repeated such reports for the remaining seven quarters. If it had been possible in GA, we would have selected a date range from January 1, 2019 through December 31, 2020, and then proceeded with one Excel worksheet.

Since we are interested in the effectiveness of First Principles of Instruction, we needed to further segment the temporal maps by views of web pages that were designed accordingly.

Since there are multiple web pages associated with each FPI (see Table 2.1 in Chapter 2), we used the GA Behavior reporting tool to do this segmenting, since we wanted to obtain counts of unique pageviews.

Using GA to Find Matches of Pageviews within Segments

After signing into the GA website for IPTAT, we selected the UA Behavior reporting tool, Site Content, All Pages. We selected the same date range for 2020 Quarter 1 and the defined segments for users who had and had not passed a Certification Test. This report is for each IPTAT web page, and there are over 100 different pages.

In order to find matches for views of pages designed with the Activation Principle, we used the search function to find matches within this overall site content report. We searched for the string, '/activation' (see Table 2.1, Chapter 2). Thus, we were able to get counts of all unique views of pages designed with the Activation Principle.

Tables 4.1 and 4.2 provide the basic information that we extracted from GA reports in order to do APT. The remainder of the process was to derive the further measures needed for APT. We used Microsoft Excel to do this, but any spreadsheet software could have been used as long as it allows formulas to generate data in cells from data in other cells.

Since we want our APT results to apply to learning journeys, we used a spreadsheet with formulas to create Table 4.3. In order to determine the mean duration per learning journey for users who had passed a Certification Test, we simply multiplied the mean number of temporal maps per learning journey by the mean time per map. For example, for those who passed we multiplied 2.74 by 00:34:43, resulting in 1:34:38 (= 94 minutes, 38 seconds). Note that the Excel spreadsheet formula we used contained numbers with greater arithmetic precision, which have been rounded to two decimal places and whole numbers of seconds in tables presented here.

Similarly, we derived the mean number of pageviews per learning journey by multiplying the mean number of temporal maps by the mean number of pageviews per map. For example, for those who passed, we multiplied 2.74 by 28.03, resulting in a mean of 76.36 pageviews per learning journey in which a Certification Test was passed.

Next, we derived the total number of pageviews of pages designed with First Principles of Instruction from Table 4.2. For those who passed a Certification Test, we summed the row cells for that segment (111,026 + . . .

52 More Details of the Big Study

Table 4.1 Basic IPTAT Audience Usage Statistics for 2020 Quarter 1: Jan. 1–Mar. 31

Segments: Learning Journeys for Users Who Have	Number of Unique Learning Journeys	Number of Temporal Maps (GA Sessions)	Temporal Maps per Learning Journey	Number of Learning Journey Pageviews	Number of Learning Journey Pageviews per Map	Mean Duration per Map (HH:MM:SS)
Passed	50,509	134,972	2.74	3,783,879	28.03	00:34:43
Not Passed	100,644	166,895	1.66	2,075,923	12.44	00:13:53
Total	151,153	301,867	2.03	5,859,802	19.41	00:23:12

Table 4.2 Unique Views of IPTAT Web Pages Designed with First Principles of Instruction for 2020 Quarter 1: Jan. 1–Mar. 31

Segments: Learning Journeys for Users Who Have	Activation	Demonstration	Application	Integration	Mastery Test	Certification Test	Adaptive Demonstration
Passed	111,026	96,089	478,005	73,919	161,523	81,612	165,544
Not Passed	53,880	50,631	221,927	34,500	78,506	39,883	74,527
Total	164,906	146,720	699,932	108,419	240,029	121,495	240,071

Table 4.3 Derived Measures from Table 4.1 for 2020 Quarter 1

Segments: Learning Journeys for Users Who Have	Mean Duration per Learning Journey (HH:MM:SS)	Mean Pageviews per Learning Journey	Total Unique Pageviews of First Principles
Passed	1:34:28	76.36	1,167,718
Not Passed	0:21:15	20.53	553,854

+ 165,544 = 1,167,718); and we did likewise for those who had not passed (= 553,854 unique views of pages designed with First Principles).

We derived similar results for those user learning journeys in which they did not pass a Certification Test in Table 4.3. These results were not available in the GA Audience report. Thus, we needed to derive the measures on a per learning journey basis here.

The next step involved deriving average numbers of unique pageviews of each First Principle. For example, for the Activation Principle for the segment of those who had passed a Certification Test, we converted it to a proportion (111,026/1,167,718 = 0.095) and then multiplied that by the mean number of pages viewed by that segment (0.095 × 76.36 = 7.26). What this means is that in successful student learning journeys, they viewed on

More Details of the Big Study 53

Table 4.4 Mean Unique Views of IPTAT Web Pages per Learning Journey that Were Designed with First Principles of Instruction for 2020 Quarter 1

Segments: Learning Journeys for Users Who Have	Activation	Demonstration	Application	Integration	Mastery Test	Certification Test	Adaptive Demonstration
Passed	7.26	6.28	31.26	4.83	10.56	5.34	10.83
Not Passed	2.00	1.88	8.23	1.28	2.91	1.48	2.76
Odds Ratio (P:NP)	3.63	3.35	3.80	3.78	3.63	3.61	3.92

average 7.26 unique IPTAT web pages designed with the Activation Principle. On the other hand, for those who had not passed a CT, they viewed on average about 2.00 unique IPTAT web pages designed with the Activation Principle. Thus, students in learning journeys where they passed a Certification Test viewed about 3.63 times as many IPTAT *Activation* web pages (7.26/2.00) as did those in learning journeys in which a CT was not passed.

In Table 4.4, we can see that the odds ratios range from 3.35 to 3.92. We can interpret this to mean that, on average, student learning journeys in which they passed a Certification Test contained between three and four times as many unique views of web pages designed with First Principles of Instruction than they did for journeys in which no Certification Test was passed. This kind of APT analysis is an indicator of the effectiveness of FPI during 2020 Quarter 1.

Wash, Rinse, and Repeat, then Combine

Due to the GA limitation reporting of segmented data streams to a maximum of 90 days, we needed to repeat the above process for seven more sets of Tables similar to 4.1 through 4.4, one set for each quarter. In our Excel spreadsheet, we created separate worksheets for each quarter. These worksheets used the same formulas as described above for derived measures needed for APT. Then we combined these results into an overall worksheet for all eight quarters in 2019 and 2020. In effect, this is how we obtained results reported in Chapter 2, Tables 2.2 and 2.3.

Some Key Issues We Identified and Resolved to do APT of IPTAT Data Streams Created by GA

One of the important considerations in using Google Analytics is to understand how GA determines unique users. Normally, we think of a unique person as an individual person, such as each of the authors of this book.

Each person may have additional identifiers associated with them such as their first and last name, driver's license number (if any), social security number (if any), the primary address where the person lives, photographs of the individual, and so forth. In GA, the primary identifier is what is referred to in GA reports as the "client ID", which is a unique hashed number that is stored in a browser cookie. This is normally a reasonably good indicator of a unique person, if they use the same browser to access the IPTAT website from occasion to occasion (and do not have browser settings or other software which prevents tracking via browser cookies). When that person uses the same device and browser at a different time, GA tracking methods invoked when an IPTAT web page is viewed check for the existence of that GA cookie, and use the client ID stored in the cookie. This is the main method used in Universal Analytics, and how users are identified in our Big Study when doing Analysis of Patterns in Time. Our IPTAT software does *not* send any additional information to GA on user identities.

On the other hand, IPTAT does identify unique users when they register in order to take a Certification Test. To do so, a person is required to supply their e-mail address and at minimum their first and last name. We implemented this feature into IPTAT in August 2014, in order to address instructor concerns of how students had been cheating on the IPTAT (see Frick et al., 2018). Attempts to register to take IPTAT tests are recorded in our own separate MySQL database at Indiana University. IPTAT requires users to then confirm their registration by going to the e-mail account registered and click on an embedded link that returns them to IPTAT and supplies a unique activation code. Thus, our MySQL records at Indiana University identify users by their e-mail address and other information they supply when registering. Most importantly, if a user passes one of the Certification Tests, the date and time when this occurs and the unique test ID are further stored in the MySQL record associated with their unique e-mail address. Since we have implemented this method of record keeping, instructors have stopped complaining to us about counterfeit Certificates, since there is now a way for them to independently check on the Certificate's validity (see https://plagiarism.iu.edu/certificationTests/certificateValidation.html). This method also allows students to login at a later date and retrieve their Certificate in order to send it to themselves or their instructor, as well as to print the Certificate if desired.

The main point we emphasize here is that GA tracking methods and IPTAT data storage methods are *independent*. Moreover, GA tracks user behavior on all web pages which are viewed, whereas IPTAT only records when users register, confirm their registration, and login and pass Certification Tests.

Where there is overlap, we have a way to confirm the relative accuracy of Google tracking. If and only if a user passes a Certification Test and they click on the button to mail their Certificate is one of two pageviews possible ('/mailCertificateUG.php' or '/mailCertificateGR.php'). We wondered how well these independent data sources agree?

If we use GA reports on unique pageviews of the 'mailCertificate*.php' scripts, we have found relatively close agreement between these independent sources. The number of unique pageviews is a relatively small underestimate. For example, in the Big Study in 2019 and 2020, the GA report of unique pageviews of the mailed Certificates is 308,039 which is less than 315,376 users who passed a CT in our MySQL records during the same interval. Thus, the GA unique pageviews of 'mailCertificate*.php' scripts is about 2 percent less than the actual number of registered users in our MySQL database who passed a CT.

Why is there any discrepancy between these independent data sources? The simple answer is that some students who pass a test do *not* click on the button to mail their Certificate. GA tracking methods will not record a pageview of '/mailCertificate*.php' unless the user clicks on the button to do so. It is also possible that IPTAT users have set their devices to prevent GA tracking from recording which pages they view, which would also account for the relatively small GA underestimate of passed CTs.

What if a user passes more than one CT? While this is certainly a possibility, it rarely occurs. We know this from yet a further independent data source. Our PHP scripts also record a line of data in our Certificate log whenever a test is passed. Having examined these logs over the past five years, we know this is a rare event where someone from the same e-mail address has more than one Certificate with different test IDs. It is not uncommon that users will mail their same unique Certificate to themselves more than once—we do see this in our Certificate log. However, in our MySQL database, we only store when the most recent CT is passed, so there is only one record per user e-mail. And that is why in GA we focus on *unique* pageviews by users.

What about users who change devices from one session to the next? We know that this does occur from time to time. A GA 'session' is defined by interaction with IPTAT web pages with the time between pageviews to be less than 30 minutes (a default for GA). If the same person returns to IPTAT using a different device or browser, GA, as we have implemented it in Universal Analytics (UA), will assign a different client ID to the new session via their tracking methods. This is why we refer to *unique learning journeys* when doing APT in our Big Study as reported here. While there is good correspondence between different users and different learning journeys, it is not perfect, since the same user can change devices or browsers between GA sessions. And furthermore, different users can share the same device and browser, and would therefore appear to GA tracking as the same user and be assigned the same client ID. While these situations may be viewed as a limitation to GA tracking methods in UA reports, this limitation does need to be recognized.

And because the large majority of users who take IPTAT Certification Tests pass only one test each, we do have clear data to support the congruence between GA tracking and our IPTAT MySQL records—even though GA tracking reports contain relatively small underestimates from the actual number of registered IPTAT users who pass a CT. When there are such large numbers of users and learning journeys, these minor discrepancies do not appreciably change the reported odds ratios. What is remarkable is the consistency we have observed from quarter to quarter in 2019 and 2020. Also noteworthy is that we have observed similar patterns for the past five years, although we report here only on the effectiveness of First Principles of Instruction in the Big Study over the past two years.

The other fact to keep in mind is that IPTAT has no records about users who do not register and login to take tests, whereas GA tracking does include these non-registrants. This is another reason we prefer to do APT on a *per learning journey* basis, when comparing patterns of pageviews for those who have passed a CT with patterns for those who have not. Some users never register for IPTAT and thus by definition cannot pass a Certification Test. These users nonetheless do have IPTAT learning journeys, even though they may be "dabblers" as discussed in Chapter 3.

Finally, we have been discussing what we did in the Big Study with Universal Analytics. In October 2020 Google formally introduced GA4, which implements many improvements to UA. Since GA4 will continue to evolve over time, what we note as current limitations of UA may not apply to GA4. One area to consider carefully is how users are identified. GA4 already incorporates what Google calls 'signals' to identify unique users across multiple sessions and apps (e.g., see https://support.google.com/analytics/answer/9445345?hl=en and https://www.blog.google/products/marketingplatform/analytics/new_google_analytics/). While web browser cookies were used in UA for our Big Study in order to determine client IDs, cookies may or may not be one of the potential signals that GA4 uses in the future. We note that "digital fingerprinting" methods are already being used at websites which attempt to identify unique users (e.g., see Frick, 2020, pp. 696–699). This further raises the issue of user privacy, which we address explicitly in IPTAT at: https://plagiarism.iu.edu/privacy.html.

Can You Do APT with GA4?

The short answer is yes, but you should pay careful attention to what is being counted.

More Details of the Big Study 57

In exploring differences between UA and GA4, we set up GA4 tracking for IPTAT in early December 2020. We have since begun to explore how we could also do APT with GA4 tracking methods and analytical tools. We have used essentially the same APT strategy of segmenting and matching in order to get the types of pattern counts we wanted from temporal maps.

There are several key differences between UA and GA4. A central concept in GA4 is the recording of an 'event' when tracking users. GA4 methods can further be used with apps (i.e., not just using a web browser). Events can include pageviews in web browsers as in UA, but now also many other things that GA4 can track: user purchasing of a product, scrolling, clicking, viewing a screen in the app, etc. With UA, events were limited to web pageviews and several other events generated by web browsers (e.g., playing a movie, executing JavaScript within the web page, etc.).

Second, GA4 tracks user engagement somewhat more precisely—not only time spent on a page, but also tracks user scrolling and determines whether the web page is in focus or not (e.g., when a user switches away from their browser window and returns later). Furthermore, GA4 counts 'engaged sessions' separately from 'sessions' themselves. And 'views' are both views of screen displays in apps as well as views of web pages (pageviews). Each 'view' event is tracked, as well as other events—even if they are repeated within a session.

One thing GA4 makes relatively easy to do is to create new kinds of events, called 'conversion events' (or goals achieved). This was possible in UA, but we had only done so recently in the Big Study and have not reported this here. We took the opportunity in GA4 to define new conversion events that are associated with First Principles of Instruction in early December 2020. For example, we defined an 'Activation' event as a conversion that occurred whenever one of the IPTAT activation pages was viewed. Similarly, we defined 'Demonstration', 'Application', etc., conversion events. We also defined an event when a user passes an undergraduate Certification Test, as well as one when they pass a graduate level CT.

Once these goals (GA 'conversions') were defined and their tracking was enabled in early December 2020, then these conversion events were also tracked by GA4 and subsequently became available for analysis with GA4 reporting tools. For example, we can now see in real-time in GA4 how many times in the past 30 minutes an Activation goal was achieved, or an Undergraduate CT was passed.

In order to evaluate the effectiveness of FPI between December 20 and January 18, we used the GA4 Explore 'Analysis Hub' and selected the 'Segment Overlap' tool. We could only do this on tracking data collected *after* GA4 was initiated for the IPTAT website, not during the previous two-year Big Study.

We defined a segment for passing a CT by creating a segment for users when the page path contains '/mail' at any point. We defined a similar segment for *not* passing a CT by creating a segment to permanently exclude users when page path contains '/mail' at any point. This effectively separated user learning journeys into two *mutually exclusive groups*.

Next, we added a dimension for breakdowns, 'is conversion event', and selected values for 'active users', 'conversions', and 'event count per user'. This resulted in a report that is summarized in Table 4.5.

As can be seen in Table 4.5, there were learning journeys for 9,471 active users, who viewed FPI web pages 2,006,689 times. This means that students who passed an IPTAT CT viewed, on average, 211.9 FPI pages per learning journey (2,006,689 divided by 9,471). On the other hand, students who did not pass an IPTAT CT viewed an average of 39.1 FPI pages per learning journey. The odds ratio is 5.41, which means that, on average, students who passed a CT viewed 5.41 times as many web pages designed with First Principles of Instruction per learning journey than did students who did not pass a CT.

While this odds ratio is somewhat higher than we reported for FPI in the Big Study, you should note that in the former, we were considering *unique views* of web pages designed with First Principles (as discussed earlier), whereas here with GA4 we effectively considered *total* pageviews in Table 4.5. That is, whenever a web page designed with FPI was viewed it was counted in GA4 as a goal event, even if repeated within a GA session. Had we reported total pageviews using UA in the Big Study in Chapter 2, the odds ratios would have been higher also as we observed here with GA4.

GA4 has additional capabilities that support APT beyond what we briefly demonstrated in this example, which we have kept simple for purposes of illustration. The main advantage of GA4 is that it can combine tracking that is done via apps that run on client devices in addition to web browsers, whereas UA was limited to tracking website usage.

Table 4.5 APT via GA4 Segmenting: First Principles of Instruction Goals Achieved in IPTAT between December 20, 2020 and January 18, 2021

Segment	Active Users (Learning Journeys)	FPI Conversions (Goals Achieved)	FPI Conversions (Goals) per Learning Journey
Passed	9,471	2,006,689	211.9
Not Passed	24,462	1,005,826	39.1
Odds Ratio (P:NP)	0.368	1.995	5.41

Who Are the Registered IPTAT Users in 2019 and 2020 (from Our MySQL Database at IU)?

When users register for IPTAT, there is a checkbox where they do or do not give us permission to use any of their data—in aggregate form only. Therefore, as we provide summary results below, we exclude data from users in 2019 and 2020 who have not given us permission during IPTAT registration. Moreover, we do not attempt to explicitly link data from GA and MySQL reports in order to respect user privacy. Of those 381,724 student users who activated their registrations in the Big Study, 352,654 gave us permission to use their data when they registered for IPTAT (about 92 percent of the registrants).

As can be seen in Figure 4.1, for those 343,012 registrants who reported their age when registering, the large majority (about 75 percent) were between ages 18 and 29. This is not surprising since we originally expected our primary target audiences for IPTAT to be undergraduate and graduate students. What we noticed in 2016, however, was that some students at the high school level and occasionally in middle school were using our IPTAT to learn about plagiarism. In Figure 4.1, note that about 9 percent of the registrants reported that they were between 14 and 17 years old. Note also that about 17 percent reported that they were 30 years of age or older.

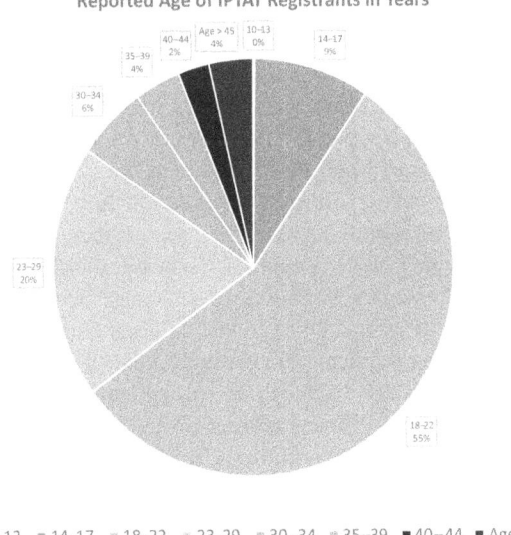

Figure 4.1 Reported Age of Registrants in Years: IPTAT 2019–2020

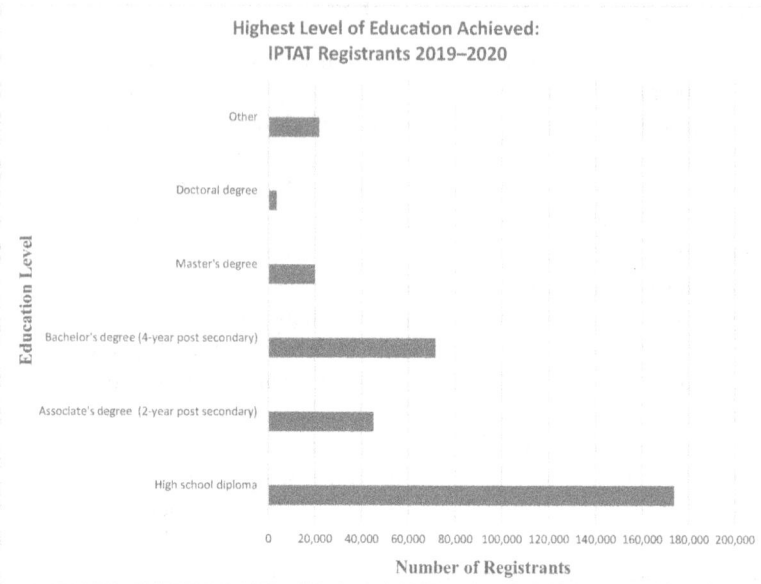

Figure 4.2 Highest Level of Education Achieved: IPTAT 2019–2020

During IPTAT registration, users are asked to indicate the highest level of education achieved. As can be seen in Figure 4.2, slightly over half (52 percent) indicated that their highest degree was a high school diploma. Another 13 percent reported that they had completed two years of postsecondary education (or an associate's degree). Thus, about 65 percent are likely to be in an undergraduate program or have an associate's degree. On the other hand, 21 percent reported that they had achieved a bachelor's degree; thus, these are likely students who are pursuing master's degrees. Noteworthy is that about 6 percent selected the "other" category. Most of these registrants indicated that they were still in high school, and some indicated that they were pursuing some kind of post-bachelor's degree certificate. However, the large majority of IPTAT users (about 93 percent) indicated that they were undergraduate or graduate students.

During registration for IPTAT, users are asked, "Why are you considering this tutorial?" As can be seen in Figure 4.3, about 94 percent report that "it is an assignment or requirement by my teacher or school". About 5 percent indicate that they are just curious or want to learn about plagiarism.

Finally, we ask on the IPTAT survey during registration, "How would you rate your current level of understanding of what plagiarism is?" As can be seen in Figure 4.4, only about 3 percent of the registrants reported "little

More Details of the Big Study   61

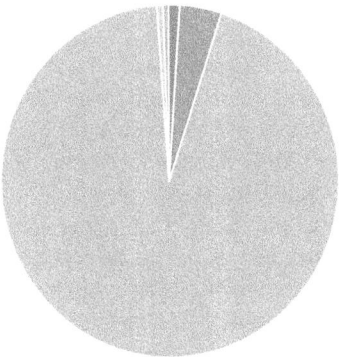

Figure 4.3 Why Are You Considering This Tutorial? IPTAT 2019–2020

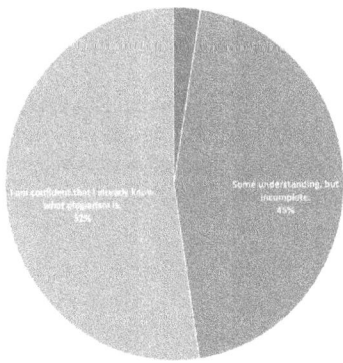

Figure 4.4 Current Levels of Understanding Plagiarism: IPTAT 2019–2020

or none" while over half indicated "I am confident that I already know what plagiarism is".

Summary

In this chapter we provided greater detail about the Big Study of the Indiana University Plagiarism Tutorials and Tests (IPTAT) for data collected in 2019 and 2020. We described the basic strategies used in doing Analysis of Patterns in Time (APT) through leveraging ways of segmenting and matching via Google Analytics (GA) reporting tools. Then we extracted results from GA reports and inserted them into a spreadsheet, which then did further calculations in order to derive the proper APT counts of temporal patterns. Finally, we have described basic user characteristics for those who registered for our IPTAT in order to take Certification Tests. This chapter elaborates earlier descriptions provided in Chapters 2 and 3.

References

Frick, T. W. (1983). *Nonmetric temporal path analysis: An alternative to the linear models approach for verification of stochastic educational relations* [Unpublished doctoral dissertation]. Indiana University Graduate School.

Frick, T. W. (1990). Analysis of patterns in time (APT): A method of recording and quantifying temporal relations in education. *American Educational Research Journal, 27*(1), 180–204.

Frick, T. W. (2020). Education systems and technology in 1990, 2020, and beyond. *TechTrends*. https://doi.org/10.1007/s11528-020-00527-y

Frick, T. W., & Dagli, C. (2016). MOOCs for research: The case of the Indiana University plagiarism tutorials and tests. *Technology, Knowledge and Learning, 21*(2), 255–276.

Frick, T. W., Dagli, C., Kwon, K., & Tomita, K. (2018). Indiana University plagiarism tutorials and tests: 14 Years of worldwide learning online. In B. Hokanson et al. (Eds.), *Educational technology and narrative: Story and instructional design* (Chapter 16, pp. 191–205). Springer.

5 Analysis of Patterns in Time as a Research Methodology

Summary: We discuss APT in greater detail. We first provide several historical examples of use of APT as a research method. We then describe use of APT concepts outside of educational research. One example is *Moneyball*, which is the story of how the Oakland Athletics professional baseball team used sabermetrics in evaluating players. This helped the Oakland A's field winning teams at a fraction of the cost of player salaries paid by other successful Major League Baseball teams. The second example is Google Analytics, which provides a Web tracking service to help their business clients determine advertising strategies and patterns of usage that lead to increased sales of the clients' products and services.

Introduction

As indicated in Chapter 1, APT does not fit within standard state-trait approaches, especially quantitative linear models, nor does it fit within standard qualitative methods which often result in narratives and rich descriptions of unique cases and phenomena. APT requires the creation of temporal maps. Such maps document events dynamically, and hence can describe processes. Temporal maps can represent learning journeys, which is the focus of this book.

Over the past four decades a number of studies have demonstrated the value of APT (An, 2003; Barrett, 2015; Dagli, 2017; Frick, 1983, 1990, 1992; Frick et al., 2008; 2009; 2010; Howard et al., 2010; Koh, 2008; Koh & Frick, 2009; Lara, 2013; Luk, 1994; Myers, 2012; Myers & Frick, 2015; Plew, 1989; Yin, 1998). A comprehensive description of APT with examples is provided in Myers and Frick (2015); we will not repeat those details here.

We focus on APT examples in the remainder of this chapter, first by reviewing three educational research studies which empirically demonstrate how APT can be used and adapted. Then we turn our attention to two

DOI: 10.4324/9781003176343-05

APT of Direct Instruction and Academic Learning Time: Joint Event Occurrences

In the first major study to compare APT with linear models (Frick, 1990, p. 25), mildly disabled children were observed throughout the day in their elementary school classroom learning environments in central and southern Indiana. Each child was observed between 8 and 10 hours across multiple days over a semester. These environments ranged from self-contained classrooms for special education students to regular classrooms in which the mildly disabled children were included. Trained classroom observers coded the kinds of academic learning activities provided, and within each reading and mathematics activity the behaviors of target students and instruction made available to the student were coded at 1-minute intervals. During data analysis, student behaviors at each time sampling point were collapsed into two categories: engagement (EN) and non-engagement (NE). Similarly, instructional behaviors at each sampling point were collapsed into two categories: direct interactive instruction (DI) and non-direct non-interactive instruction (ND).

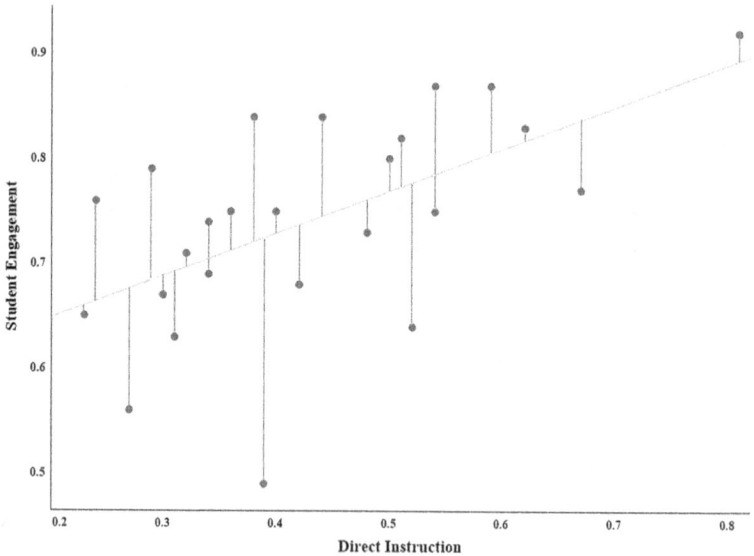

Figure 5.1 The Linear Models Approach to Analyzing a Relation. Regression equation: $EN = 0.40DI + 0.57$. $R^2 = 0.33$.

Linear Models Approach

As can be seen in Figure 5.1, if the data are analyzed with the linear models approach (LMA), student engagement can be predicted by a regression equation. Approximately 33 percent of the variance in student engagement can be accounted for by the amount of direct instruction provided. While this finding shows that there is a statistically significant positive relationship ($p < 0.05$) that is moderate in size, there is still a great deal of uncertainty (67 percent of the variance is not predictable). Notice that the vertical lines indicate the distances between the data points in the scatterplot and the regression line, indicating *errors* in prediction. The relationship between direct instruction and engagement is represented by a function for a line. In this example, the function for the line is: *EN = 0.57 + 0.40DI*. Each data point represents the overall proportion of engagement (EN) for a particular student, paired with the overall proportion of direct instruction (DI) provided to that student. EN is aggregated *separately* from DI for each case, so there is one overall EN score for a student and one overall DI score. Thus, there are 25 data pairs from which the regression equation is estimated. In Table 5.1, columns 2 and 3 respectively contain p(DI) and p(EN) for each student. For example, for student 1, p(DI) = 0.50 and p(EN) = 0.80, which is one of the (x,y) data pairs in Figure 5.1.

APT Approach

The same data were analyzed from an APT perspective. From this perspective data are aggregated differently. The *joint occurrences* of student engagement and instruction were counted in order to form probabilities or proportions. For example, for student 1, the *joint probability* of DI and EN occurring is p(DI ∩ EN) = 0.46; p(DI ∩ NE) = 0.04. The *conditional* probability of EN occurring given that DI is occurring is p(EN | DI) = 0.92; and p(EN | ND) = 0.67. These joint (denoted by ∩) and conditional (denoted by |) probability estimates for this student were based on nearly 500 data points where the joint occurrences of instruction and engagement were observed and coded. Similar probabilities were estimated for the remaining 24 students, and then the probabilities were averaged. Thus, there were nearly 15,000 data points representing the joint occurrences of direct instruction and engagement for the 25 students. See Table 5.1.

As can be seen in the two far-right columns in Table 5.1, conditional probabilities for student engagement during direct instruction and non-direct instruction are presented. The mean probability of student engagement during direct instruction is very high (0.967). Students are about 1.7 times more likely to be engaged during direct instruction than during non-direct instruction (0.967/0.573). Another way to look at this is the likelihood

Table 5.1 Temporal Relationships of Teacher Instruction and Student Engagement

Student	p(DI)	p(EN)	p(DI ∩ EN)	p(DI ∩ NE)	p(ND ∩ EN)	p(ND ∩ NE)	p(EN|DI)	p(EN|ND)
1	0.50	0.80	0.46	0.04	0.34	0.16	0.92	0.67
2	0.39	0.49	0.37	0.02	0.12	0.49	0.95	0.20
3	0.27	0.56	0.26	0.01	0.30	0.43	0.97	0.41
4	0.34	0.69	0.34	0.00	0.35	0.31	1.00	0.53
5	0.48	0.73	0.47	0.01	0.25	0.26	0.98	0.49
6	0.40	0.75	0.39	0.01	0.35	0.25	0.98	0.59
7–25	...	...	...	...	...	...	...	...
Mean	**0.432**	**0.741**	**0.416**	**0.015**	**0.324**	**0.243**	**0.967**	**0.573**
(SD)	(0.144)	(0.101)	(0.139)	(0.010)	(0.114)	(0.104)	(0.029)	(0.142)

Source: Adapted from Table 1 (Frick, 1990). Joint Occurrences of Direct Instruction (DI), Student Engagement (EN), Non-direct Instruction (ND), and Student Non-engagement (NE) in Columns 4–7; Conditional Occurrences in Columns 8–9.

of non-engagement during non-direct instruction. Students are about 12.9 times more likely to be off-task during non-direct instruction (($1-0.573$)/($1-0.967$)). These patterns are very clear and consistent across 25 different students. When teachers interacted with those target students either individually or in groups that included those students, they were very likely to be on-task. These probability ratios (odds) are *in principle* no different than the odds of getting some kind of cancer later in life being between five and ten times greater for heavy smokers, when compared with non-smokers (Kumar et al., 2005). This temporal relationship is not necessarily causal, but nonetheless is a predictable pattern.

APT of Teacher-Student Interaction in Class: Frequency of Sequential Events

Koh (2008) investigated how teachers in educational technology classes used scaffolding strategies. Scaffolding is one of the strategies that is often discussed in problem-based learning methods, as well as in instructional design for complex learning (cf. van Merriënboer & Kirschner, 2007; van Merriënboer et al., 2002). She videotaped university classes for about 27 hours. She then coded the videotapes using the classifications which are the column headings in Map 5.1. To protect identities of students, their names have been changed to capital letters (C, H, L and M in this sample extracted from one of the classes she observed).

A particular pattern has been highlighted in Map 5.1 for purposes of illustration. Koh (2008) was interested in mapping the temporal sequences but not durations of events, so there is no classification for date and time in

APT as a Research Methodology   67

Map 5.1 Coding Example Adapted from Joyce Koh's Dissertation (2008, p. 38)

Temporal Order	Instructional Activity	From	To	Student Interaction	Instructor Interaction	Resources	Equipment
1	Lab	Instructor	C	Null	Null	Project/ Assignment descriptions	Student computer terminal
2					Show & tell		
3		C	Instructor	Clarify task			
4		Instructor	C		Direction maintenance		
5		C	Instructor	Tech help			
6		Instructor	C		Show & tell †		
7		C	Instructor	Clarify content			
8		Instructor	C		Direction maintenance		
9					Frustration control		
10					Direction maintenance		
11		M	Instructor	Can't hear	Can't hear		
12		Instructor	M				
13		L	Instructor	Tech help			
14		Instructor	L		Progress check ø		
15					Show & tell †		
16		H	Instructor	Tech help			
17		Instructor	H		Progress check ø		
18		H	Instructor	Share content			
19		Instructor	H		Show & tell		
20		L	Instructor	Tech help			
21		Instructor	L		Show & tell †		

Note: Cell entries have been highlighted to indicate instances of the pattern for APT Query: If Student Interaction is Tech help, then Instructor Interaction is Show & tell?

Map 5.1. Each time a new event is observed, a new row is added; thus, sequence in time runs from top to bottom of the temporal map. When an event is observed in one classification, it is assumed to continue until another relevant event is observed. For example, the Instructional Activity was initially coded as *Lab*, and that activity did not change during the observation, while 13 *Instructor Interactions* were observed.

The coded instructional sequences were also used to make APT queries about the joint probabilities of categories within and between classifications. For example, to find out how instructors responded to student requests for *Tech help*, the following APT query could be formed:

> IF Student Interaction is *Tech help*, THEN Instructor Interaction is *Show & tell*?

Using the information in Map 5.1, note that there were four instances of student requests for *Tech help*. Given that *Tech help* was true, it was followed three times by *Show & tell* and two times by *Progress check*. Therefore, if students asked for *Tech help*, the probability of this instructor responding by *Show & tell* was 3/5 = 0.60. The symbol † has been added to the map to show where the APT query is true, and the symbol ø was added to show where the APT query is false in the map.

Koh and Frick (2009) present a summary of findings on patterns of classroom practice that were associated with students' computer self-efficacy. These patterns were derived from analysis of teacher and student interactions as illustrated in Map 5.1.

APT of Asynchronous Online Discussion: Sequential Patterns of Comments

Howard et al. (2010) investigated how conditions of anonymity promoted peer feedback in a pre-service teacher technology course. In-service teachers regularly need to give feedback to students about the quality of their performance or work. Consequently, the ability to give feedback is a useful skill to develop among pre-service teachers. One way to develop feedback skills is via peer feedback activities. Peer feedback can provide authentic practice opportunities for giving feedback and enhance learning beyond the development of feedback skills (Ertmer et al., 2007; Shute, 2008). However, the substance and tone of peer feedback may be influenced by perceived social consequences, both positive and negative, of the peer feedback authored. As such, anonymous feedback has been recommended as an approach to enable peer feedback with less concern for perceived social consequences.

APT as a Research Methodology   69

Howard et al. (2010) used APT to address three questions about the use of anonymity in peer feedback activities: (1) To what extent does anonymity promote or deter students from providing feedback? (2) How does the substance of feedback comments differ when students are anonymous? (3) How do critical feedback patterns differ when students are anonymous?

In this naturalistic study, 71 undergraduate students in five sections of an education technology course had built their own websites outside of class. During a subsequent in-class activity held in a computer lab, students independently commented on each other's websites in an asynchronous web forum available through the university's learning management system (LMS).

In two sections of the course, students remained anonymous during their critiques of peer websites ($n = 35$). In those classes, when a student read comments about their own website, the identities of the commentors were masked.

In the remaining three sections of the course, identities of their peers were *not* masked ($n = 37$), as would normally occur in online asynchronous discussions. Each of those students could see the real names of peers who critiqued their website.

Student feedback comments were extracted from the university LMS and imported in Microsoft Excel for analysis. Comments were divided into utterances of semantic meaning according to computer-mediated discourse analysis guidelines (Herring, 2004). Key data such as the comment author, to whom the feedback was directed, timestamps, and the sequence of the utterances within a comment were preserved within the spreadsheet. Each utterance was coded based on substance (reactionary, constructive, clarifying a standard, or null/no substance) and tenor (positive, negative, or neutral/null). Frequencies of two specific feedback patterns across the two conditions were counted through the use of Excel formulas: (1) a negative reaction followed by a constructive utterance of any tone and (2) a positive reaction followed by either a negative reaction or constructive utterance of any tone.

Locating the feedback patterns presented challenges. In looking for these two specific feedback patterns the comment timestamp was not informative, since all utterances within a comment shared the same timestamp. However, the utterances did occur in a particular temporal sequence and this sequence could be leveraged. Map 5.2 provides a snippet from a simplified spreadsheet to illustrate how feedback patterns of interest were identified and counted.

The last column of the spreadsheet (column I) includes cells that contain an Excel formula that looks for a particular feedback pattern—positive reaction then critical feedback. If the pattern was found (Pattern 2), the cell value was set to 1. If not, the cell value was set to 0. Later these counts were aggregated by a further Excel formula that used the SUM function.

70   APT as a Research Methodology

In Map 5.2, cell I3 displays a value of 1 because the pattern of feedback of a positive reaction followed by either a negative reaction or constructive utterance of any tone was found across the current and preceding rows/utterances. The full Excel formula in cell I3 for determining if Pattern 2 occurs is provided below.

$$= IF(AND(G2 = \text{``r''}, H2 = \text{``p''}, G3 = \text{``c''}, D3 = D2+1), 1, 0)$$

This formula evaluated if several conditions were true using data in the *same* row/utterance and the *previous* row/utterance. The previous row (row 2) contained an utterance (E2) coded as a positive reaction (H2 = "p" and G2 = "r"). The utterance in the same row (E3) was coded as critical substance (G3 = "c"). The sequence number of the utterance in the same row (D3) must be equal to the sequence number of the utterance in the previous row (D2) plus one. The use of 'AND' in the Excel formula meant that all the conditions listed needed to be true in order to return the 1 result; otherwise, a 0 result was returned.

Map 5.2 Simplified Excel Spreadsheet to Illustrate Feedback Pattern Identification and Counting

	A	B	C	D	E	G	H	I
1	Target	Author	Time	Seq#	Utterance	Substance	Tenor	Pattern 2
2	11	10	14:36	1	Great topic!	r	p	0
3	11	10	14:36	2	I would consider making some of the text on your content page stand out a little more, since it all seems to be just one big blob.	c	0	1
4	12	10	14:38	1	Some of the pictures were too big to see the whole image on the screen.	r	n	0
5	12	10	14:38	2	I'd also consider moving some of the text away from left alignment for some variation.	c	0	0

This was how the APT query was operationalized in Excel. Once the cell formula was created, the investigators leveraged Excel's ability to modify the formula automatically for thousands of other similar cells, by use of Excel's copy and paste capabilities. If not for this automation, the patterns would have needed to be hand counted, as did Koh (2008), such as in Map 5.1.

Rows 4 and 5 in Map 5.2 show an example of the other feedback pattern that was the focus of Howard et al. (2010) study—a negative reaction followed by a constructive utterance of any tone. The cell I5 displayed 0 because that cell was looking for the pattern previously discussed. A different column in the spreadsheet (not illustrated in Map 5.2) and a different but similarly structured Excel formula were used to operationalize the APT query to search for this pattern in the data.

Using this APT approach, Howard et al. (2010) found that:

> Students who were anonymous were approximately five times more likely to provide substantively critical feedback than were those whose identities were known to their recipients. When feedback was given anonymously, students were approximately four times more likely to provide reasons for needed improvement to a website, and then to suggest design alternatives.
>
> (p. 89)

While this example of making APT queries with Excel spreadsheet formulas is rather detailed, the main points here are that:

- Investigators coded student comments in the asynchronous online discussion according to substance and tenor of their utterances.
- Investigators inserted these codes into a temporal map, as illustrated in Map 5.2 (for different examples, see Map 5.1, as well as temporal maps in Chapter 2).
- Since investigators created each temporal map as an Excel spreadsheet, they were able to creatively devise cell formulas to carry out APT queries for segmenting and matching patterns in the maps.

This example is very similar to the one in Chapter 4 from the Big Study, where Excel cell formulas were used to derive further APT query results from the counts extracted from GA reports. The difference in Howard et al. (2010)'s study is that the *investigators* parsed the student online comments and hand-coded them according to a category scheme relevant to the focus of the research.

Alternatively, in the 2019–2020 Big Study, GA had already stored the sequences of individual student interaction with IPTAT by tracking their pageviews. The classification and coding of student behavior was subsequently facilitated by using GA reporting tools to do the segmenting and matching to derive results needed for each APT query. Thus, both GA and Excel were leveraged in the Big Study in order to do APT.

See Howard et al. (2010) for further details of how APT helped answer their research questions.

We now turn to two examples of APT outside of education: *Moneyball* and Google Analytics.

APT Outside of Education

Moneyball

Lewis (2004) described a different approach to collecting information about prospective players for Major League Baseball (MLB) in the United States. This approach was kept secret for some time because it gave teams who used it a competitive advantage. Lewis tells the story of how the Oakland Athletics organization was able to field teams who won enough baseball games to make it to the playoffs at the end of the season, some going on to the World Series.

The problem was that after professional baseball players were permitted to become free agents, they could essentially market themselves to the highest bidders for contracts, salaries, and benefits. This drove up the costs significantly for team owners. Lewis reports that in 2002 the New York Yankees spent approximately $126 million on player salaries, compared with the Oakland Athletics, who spent about $40 million. The prevailing strategy was to hire the best players, who were paid the highest salaries, in order to win more games and championships. While this is capitalism in economic terms, it created considerable inequities between the richest and poorest teams. Oakland had suffered a losing season after the ownership changed in 1995. The new owners were unwilling to lose money year-in and year-out, as had the previous owner, who had a more philanthropic view towards support of the Athletics baseball team.

The general manager at that time, Billy Beane, a former professional player himself, started to ask questions about what predicted winning of games. The usual statistics that were collected were not especially good predictors, such as a player's batting average, runs batted in, homeruns, etc. This is the kind of information that is often reported in box scores by newspapers—a table that summarizes performance for each player in a game. Too many prospective players with good statistics in the box-score sense did not later turn out to be successful MLB players. How could you improve the odds, waste less money, and win more games?

The answers were surprising and went against some of the traditional baseball wisdom at the time. To make a long story short, the Oakland Athletics had been tracking what happened *during* games and discovered better statistics—identifying measures that predicted what made the biggest difference for winning games over an entire season. According to Lewis (2004), the statistician who worked for the A's, Paul DePodesta, had verified that a team's overall on-base percentage when combined with their slugging percentage[1] was a better predictor of how many games MLB teams had won historically. Finding inexpensive players who were better at getting on base more often was a key component of the A's overall strategy. *Getting on base*—whatever it took—included base hits, walks, getting hit by pitches, and hitting balls that resulted in defensive fielding errors. Teams who were more likely to get their players on base (i.e., not make an out when batting) did not necessarily have the best batting averages. But *teams with better on-base and slugging percentages were more likely to win more games*—year in and year out.

In the game of baseball, winning is defined by scoring more runs than the opposing team, normally after a minimum of nine innings are played. Each team continues to bat during each inning until the opposing team gets three outs. And by the rules, getting an 'out' occurs when the opposing team *prevents* the batting team from increasing the number of players on base for each time at bat. The batting team cannot score runs unless they get on base. Players on the other team then get their turn at batting until they make three outs during that inning. Then a new inning starts. Not making an out when a player is at-bat, that is, by getting on base, is an antecedent event to their team's scoring of runs. Hitting home runs, which immediately results in scoring runs, is still getting on base, albeit very briefly. And the temporal pattern is clear: when a player gets on base, the likelihood of their team's scoring a run *before* making three outs is greater. When no players get on base during the inning, the likelihood is zero.

These new kinds of measures were called 'sabermetrics', originally pioneered in the 1970s by Bill James (2003, 2005) (see also https://en.wikipedia.org/wiki/Sabermetrics). The key difference was that in-game activity was tracked temporally and new measures were obtained, not just summary statistics from box scores. Many of these new measures were based on temporal patterns of gameplay. In effect, observers were charting games and forming what are called temporal maps in APT. Bill James referred to them as 'score sheets', according to Lewis (2004).

Notably, Frick (1990) referred to APT 'scores', using the analogy of a musical score, but later changed the nomenclature to 'temporal maps', since the term 'score' has multiple meanings in conventional language.

Google Analytics

Many features of Google Analytics (GA) utilize key ideas from Analysis of Patterns in Time. What motivated Google to invent Google Analytics appears to be a need to provide data on business marketing efforts and their relative success (Google Analytics, 2005–present). This required collecting information that would help those businesses determine how web users found their business websites and what they did once arriving at those websites. Businesses want to know what advertisements and other techniques are most effective in leading users to purchase their products or services. This goal requires sequential analysis methods once ways of tracking web users' behaviors have been established.

We note that this is very similar to Frick's (1990) original goal for APT:

> Knowledge of likelihoods of temporal patterns can be used to predict subsequent events and aid decision makers, for example, for forecasting. Although temporal patterns do not necessarily indicate causal relationships, such patterns may provide good leads to further experimental research.
>
> (p. 181)

This GA goal is also similar to what baseball insiders sought to do, initially within the Oakland Athletics organization, as Lewis (2004) described. They wanted to find out what led to winning seasons in U.S. professional baseball. Which players should they recruit and select who could be drafted or obtained through trades—to be paid salaries the owner could afford—to do the things during baseball games which mattered most for winning games against their opponents? This is also a temporal problem—looking at probabilities of earlier events which lead to later events (or trying to predict those future events). Shrewd baseball owners and general managers want to get the biggest bang for their buck, not unlike business executives and their marketing departments who want to spend their advertising budgets in the most economical ways that, in turn, maximize their sales and profits.

As educators, we also want to provide learning journeys for students which increase the odds that they will succeed—achieve the learning goals.

Fundamentally, these are all the same kind of problem: If we do X now, what are the chances that Y will happen later?

Google Analytics has evolved considerably since they purchased Urchin Software in 2005, a company which had developed WebAnalytics. We described a few current features of GA that were utilized in Chapters 2 and 4 to illustrate by example how to do APT of IPTAT data. The first author discovered in late February 2020 a way to closely approximate APT using the GA tools for segmenting and matching. *This was a huge breakthrough*, which we did not anticipate when we initially set up GA tracking in the new version of IPTAT, which was launched on January 2, 2016. It was a serendipitous discovery by the first author when playing with GA tools in late February 2020, while sequestered at home when the novel coronavirus pandemic was emerging in the U.S. Once the big "aha" moment occurred, it was off to the races to see how far Google Analytics could be pushed to do Analysis of Patterns in Time. As it turns out, GA can do a very good approximation to APT, as detailed by Myers and Frick (2015), when supplemented by a spreadsheet which uses further cell formulas to derive APT results from counts extracted from GA reports.

As mentioned in Chapter 4, starting in mid-October 2020, Google has begun replacing Universal Analytics (UA) with Google Analytics 4 (GA4). Our Big Study utilized UA tracking methods and UA reporting tools, as we illustrated in Chapters 2 and 4. In December 2020 we connected UA with GA4 tracking and analysis methods. Going forward in 2021, we will be able to use GA4 reporting tools to do APT with tracking data that has been collected in 2021 and later.

While GA4 provides further analytic tools and is organized somewhat differently than UA, GA4 still relies on segmenting and matching as before, and we will be able to do APT with GA4 reporting methods in a similar manner. We have already verified this with the new data being collected and will be able to do newer Big Studies in future research and evaluation with IPTAT and GA4.

Most importantly, the big ideas that serve as the foundation for APT have not changed since the 1970s. What has changed over the past five decades is the computer technology and available analytical software tools. As we next demonstrate in Chapters 6 and 7, we have discovered ways of adapting software tools available at those earlier times, much as we have done in the Big Study described here.

Note

1 Slugging percentage refers to the average number of bases gained for each at bat—a weighted formula that is not explained here to simplify the example.

References

An, J. (2003). *Understanding mode errors in modern human-computer interfaces: Toward the design of usable software* [Unpublished doctoral dissertation]. Indiana University Graduate School.

Barrett, A. F. (2015). *Facilitating variable-length computerized classification testing via automatic racing calibration heuristics* [Unpublished doctoral dissertation]. Indiana University Graduate School.

Dagli, C. (2017). *Relationships of first principles of instruction and student mastery: A MOOC on how to recognize plagiarism* [Unpublished doctoral dissertation]. Indiana University Graduate School.

Ertmer, P. A., Richardson, J. C., Belland, B., Camin, D., Connolly, P., & Coulthard, G. (2007). Using peer feedback to enhance the quality of student online postings: An exploratory study. *Journal of Computer-Mediated Communication, 12*(2), article 4. http://jcmc.indiana.edu/vol12/issue2/ertmer.html

Frick, T. W. (1983). *Nonmetric temporal path analysis (NTPA): An alternative to the linear models approach for verification of stochastic educational relations* [Unpublished doctoral dissertation]. Indiana University Graduate School. https://tedfrick.sitehost.iu.edu/ntpa/

Frick, T. W. (1990). Analysis of Patterns in Time (APT): A method of recording and quantifying temporal relations in education. *American Educational Research Journal, 27*(1), 180–204.

Frick, T. W., Chadha, R., Watson, C., Wang, Y., & Green, P. (2009). College student perceptions of teaching and learning quality. *Educational Technology Research and Development, 57*(5), 705–720.

Frick, T. W., Chadha, R., Watson, C., & Zlatkovska, E. (2010). Improving course evaluations to improve instruction and complex learning in higher education. *Educational Technology Research and Development, 58*(2), 115–136.

Frick, T. W., Myers, R., Thompson, K., & York, S. (2008). *New ways to measure systemic change: Map & Analyze Patterns & Structures Across Time (MAPSAT).* Featured research paper presented at the annual conference of the Association for Educational Communications & Technology, Orlando, FL. https://tedfrick.sitehost.iu.edu/MAPSATAECTOrlando2008.pdf

Google Analytics. (2005-present). Retrieved February 18, 2021, from https://en.wikipedia.org/wiki/Google_Analytics

Herring, S. C. (2004). Computer-mediated discourse analysis: An approach to researching online behavior. In S. A. Barab, R. Kling, & J. H. Gray (Eds.), *Designing for virtual communities* (pp. 338–376). Cambridge University Press.

Howard, C. D., Barrett, A. F., & Frick, T. W. (2010). Anonymity to promote peer feedback: Pre-service teachers' comments in asynchronous computer-mediated communication. *Journal of Educational Computing Research, 43*(1), 89–112.

James, B. (2003). *The new Bill James historical baseball abstract.* Free Press.

James, B. (2005, July 28). Beyond baseball. *Think Tank with B. Wattenberg.* Public Broadcasting System. http://www.pbs.org/thinktank/transcript1197.html

Koh, J. H. (2008). *The use of scaffolding in introductory technology skills instruction for preservice teachers* [Unpublished doctoral dissertation]. Indiana University Graduate School.

Koh, J. H., & Frick, T. W. (2009). Instructor and student classroom interactions during technology skills instruction for facilitating preservice teachers' computer self-efficacy. *Journal of Educational Computing Research, 40*(2), 207–224.

APT as a Research Methodology 77

Kumar, V., Abbas, A., & Fausto, N. (2005). *Robbins and Cotran pathologic basis of disease* (7th ed.). Elsevier/Saunders.

Lara, M. (2013). *Personality traits and performance in online game-based learning: Collaborative vs. individual settings* [Unpublished doctoral dissertation]. Indiana University Graduate School.

Lewis, M. (2004). *Moneyball: The art of winning an unfair game.* W. W. Norton & Co.

Luk, H.-K. (1994). *A comparison of an expert systems approach to computer adaptive testing and the three-parameter item response theory model* [Unpublished doctoral dissertation]. Indiana University Graduate School.

Myers, R. D. (2012). *Analyzing interaction patterns to verify a simulation/game model* [Unpublished doctoral dissertation]. Indiana University Graduate School.

Myers, R. D., & Frick, T. W. (2015). Using pattern matching to assess gameplay. In C. S. Loh, Y. Sheng, & D. Ifenthaler (Eds.), *Serious games analytics: Methodologies for performance measurement, assessment, and improvement* (Chapter 19, pp. 435–458). Springer.

Plew, T. (1989). *An empirical investigation of major adaptive testing methodologies and an expert systems approach* [Unpublished doctoral dissertation]. Indiana University Graduate School.

Shute, V. J. (2008). Focus on formative feedback. *Review of Educational Research, 78*(1), 153–189.

van Merriënboer, J. J. G., Clark, R. E., & de Croock, M. B. M. (2002). Blueprints for complex learning: The 4C/ID model. *Education Technology Research & Development, 50*(2), 39–64.

van Merriënboer, J. J. G., & Kirschner, P. A. (2007). *Ten steps to complex learning: A systematic approach to four-component instructional design.* Lawrence Erlbaum Associates.

Yin, R. (1998). *Dynamic learning patterns during individualized instruction* [Unpublished doctoral dissertation]. Indiana University Graduate School.

6 Using Analysis of Patterns in Time for Formative Evaluation of a Learning Design

Summary: We provide a further example of how APT has been used for improving an online simulation game. We used APT to improve the fidelity of the online Diffusion Simulation Game (DSG) by evaluating the congruence of DSG gameplay processes and outcomes with empirical research on adoption of innovations. We illustrate how APT was used to identify several inconsistencies of DSG gameplay outcomes with outcomes expected from theory and empirical research on diffusion of innovations. This then allowed us to correct several mistakes in DSG algorithms, and then to further use APT to verify that the changed algorithms did indeed improve DSG fidelity. The DSG has been played hundreds of thousands of times by more than 18,000 registrants from 2014 through 2020.

Introduction

In Chapter 5 we summarized several studies that have used APT to examine the effects of direct instruction, the impact of scaffolding strategies, and the use of anonymity during peer feedback. In this chapter, we discuss in detail the application of APT in evaluating the design of the Diffusion Simulation Game (DSG, 2002), which is based on Rogers' (1962/2003) description of diffusion of innovations (DOI) theory. To win the game, learners must apply appropriate strategies from DOI theory to move teachers toward acceptance of an educational innovation.

Well-designed simulations and games require players to constantly use what they have learned to solve authentic, situated problems (Edelson & Reiser, 2006; Huang & Johnson, 2009; Shaffer et al., 2005; Wideman et al., 2007). Findings demonstrate that the kinds of experiential learning available in simulations and games improve learners' problem-solving skills and judgment (Feinstein & Cannon, 2002). The basic premise of simulations designed for learning is that the knowledge and skills developed through the simulation experience will transfer to real-world situations. Peters et al. (1998) argued that "the extent to which this translation will be successful depends, among

DOI: 10.4324/9781003176343-06

other things, on the degree to which the game is a valid representation" (p. 22) of the real-world phenomenon.

Therefore, as with any designed learning experience, designers must evaluate their work to ensure that it provides accurate representations of that which is to be learned. We would not expect a textbook that is filled with factual errors to be effective in conveying knowledge; it would require significant effort on an instructor's part to correct the resultant misconceptions. Nor should we expect a simulation game that is poorly designed to be effective in providing the desired experience for the learner. However, software may seem to work well (i.e., produce some result without crashing) yet in fact produce results that are inconsistent with observations and theories of the real world that we desire learners to experience and understand.

Simulation Fidelity

Fidelity refers to the accuracy with which a simulation represents a real or imagined reference system (Alessi, 2000; Feinstein & Cannon, 2002; Liu et al., 2009). Reigeluth and Schwartz (1989) theorized that the most fundamental aspects of a simulation should have high fidelity, while lower fidelity is appropriate for the more superficial aspects that may otherwise lead to cognitive overload and impede learning and transfer. Some instructional situations that utilize simulations may require high physical fidelity (e.g., flight simulators) and others may require high cognitive fidelity, defined as "the degree to which the simulation faithfully represents conceptual aspects of the actual task" (FAS, 2006, p. 8). Fidelity may be examined in terms of a simulation's presentation (perceptual fidelity); the interaction of the components, including both a simulation's controls and its resulting behavior (functional fidelity); and the degree to which a simulation's underlying mathematical or logical model represents the reference system (model fidelity; Alessi, 2000; Alessi & Trollip, 2001; Reigeluth & Schwartz, 1989).

Although some researchers have studied how fidelity affects the experience and learning outcomes of using simulations, there is little guidance for determining the necessary levels of fidelity when designing a simulation (Gibbons et al., 2009). The various aspects of simulations, including detail, resolution, error, precision, sensitivity, timing, and capacity (Liu et al., 2009), may have different levels of fidelity within a given simulation (selective fidelity; Andrews et al., 1995). Those levels may even change— automatically or through learner control—if the simulation is designed for dynamic fidelity (Alessi, 2000). While high fidelity may be necessary or desirable for certain types of simulations, for example in engineering, it is not always the case for educational simulations. A simplified model helps learners "build their own mental models of the phenomena or procedures and provide them opportunities to explore, practice, test, and improve those models safely and efficiently" (Alessi & Trollip, 2001, p. 214). Maier and Grossler (2000) stated that a less detailed, more abstract simulation may be appropriate for business and economic systems that may otherwise be overwhelmingly complex.

Evaluation of Fidelity

Fidelity is difficult to measure objectively (Feinstein & Cannon, 2002), and subjective accounts of fidelity may be influenced by an array of confounding variables, including the learner's prior knowledge, experience, mood, and temperament, the environment in which the simulation is being run, and so forth. Comprehensive measurement is considered impossible because of uncertainty, the amount of information involved, complicated attributes and behaviors of reality, and human limitations (Liu et al., 2009).

The literature on simulation design refers to the assurance of model fidelity as validation and verification, which are distinct yet related processes for evaluating simulation models during different stages of the development process to ensure to the highest possible degree that a simulation accurately represents its reference system and is working properly. A commonly used description of the difference between the terms is that validation is concerned with building the right model and verification is concerned with building the model right (Balci, 1997; Pace, 2004). To provide a context for understanding this distinction, Sargent (2010) summarized a common paradigm of simulation modeling:

> The *problem entity* is the system (real or proposed), idea, situation, policy, or phenomena to be modeled; the *conceptual model* is the mathematical/logical/verbal representation (mimic) of the problem entity developed for a particular study; and the *computerized model* is the conceptual model implemented on a computer.
>
> (p. 159, emphasis in original)

Validation is intended to ensure that the conceptual model provides a reasonable representation of the problem entity (Balci, 1997; David, 2009; Pace, 2004; Sargent, 2010; Thacker et al., 2004). Because the focus of this study is verification of a computational model, we will not discuss approaches to validating a conceptual model. The interested reader is directed to Sargent (2010) for a discussion of validation techniques.

Once a conceptual model has been created (or selected) and validated to ensure that it is sufficient for the purposes of the simulation, it must be instantiated as a computational model that provides the underlying rules and functions of the simulation. This process requires translating the conceptual model into computer code. Model verification is the process of ensuring that this transformation has been done with sufficient accuracy, that is, that it has been programmed correctly and returns results consistent with those associated with the problem entity (Balci, 1997; Pace, 2004; Sargent, 2010; Thacker et al., 2004; Whitner & Balci, 1989).

Simulation designers usually utilize a combination of techniques for model verification because no single approach has been found to provide sufficient evidence of a model's accuracy (Sargent, 2010). Models of highly deterministic and predictable phenomena may require only quantitative analysis, whereas models of complex social phenomena may also require qualitative analysis (David, 2009). Simulations of social processes are complicated by the large number of parameters that must be estimated, the problem of identifying which variables determine behavior, and the difficulty in acquiring adequate empirical data (Garson, 2009; Gilbert, 2004). Even when variables and data collection are highly controlled, analysis of results can be challenging; the influence of initial conditions and the stochastic nature of social simulations may result in wide-ranging outcomes, and some rare events may not occur during testing (Axelrod, 2007; Smith, 1996). For a detailed discussion of model verification techniques and their relative merits, see Whitner and Balci (1989).

Using APT for Model Verification

The model verification method used in this study is an application of Frick's (1990) Analysis of Patterns in Time (APT). The goal is to provide quantified evidence of the accuracy of a computational model by comparing the behavior of and results from the computational model with predictions made based on the related conceptual model.

The following outline includes the major steps of the model verification procedure along with guiding questions and explanations. We recommend that a subject matter expert—ideally someone who was not closely involved in the design of the simulation—lead the verification effort. This approach is consistent with several other verification methods described in Whitner and Balci (1989).

1. Formulate the conceptual model as patterns of temporal events.
    a. What actions does the model specify or imply?
    b. What conditions influence or mediate those actions?
    c. What are the probable results of those actions?

2. Map those events to actions that may be taken in the simulation.
    a. What are the mechanisms/controls in the simulation?
    b. How can those mechanisms/controls be used, and what conditions influence or mediate their use?
    c. What are the possible outcomes?
3. Validate mappings of events to simulation actions.
    a. Review by selected experts who are knowledgeable about the conceptual model.
    b. Possible approaches (depending on the nature of the mappings) include asking experts to:
        i. Agree or disagree with mappings and provide rationale and alternatives.
        ii. Assign probabilities to possible results.
        iii. Rank order possible results.
4. Identify the data associated with those actions that are required for analysis.
    a. Specify in terms of mutually exclusive and exhaustive classifications and categories.
5. Specify the threshold of confidence (i.e., what are the required results for the model to be considered accurate?).
6. Programmatically collect and store the data.
    a. Data requirements are based on the specified classifications and categories.
7. Specify queries of the data for patterns of interest.
    a. Patterns of interest are those actions in the simulation that map to events indicated in the conceptual model.
    b. Patterns may be joint occurrences of categories and/or sequences of categories.
8. Analyze the results of queries to ascertain the probability that the computational model accurately represents the conceptual model. Depending on the type of data collected, this may require statistical analysis or a more qualitative method.

The Diffusion Simulation Game

The case selected to test the proposed method is an existing online simulation game, the Diffusion Simulation Game, which has as its primary conceptual model Rogers' (1962/2003) description of diffusion of innovations (DOI) theory (Molenda & Rice, 1979). The DSG is a simulation game in which the player takes on the role of a change agent in a junior high school. The player's objective is to persuade as many of the 22 staff members as possible to adopt an innovation—peer tutoring. To be effective, players must learn appropriate application and sequencing of available diffusion activities given adopters of various types at different points in the innovation-decision process.

The player may gather information about each staff member and also view diagrams of professional and interpersonal networks. The player may also choose from a variety of diffusion activities, some of which target a single individual or up to five people. For example, the player may use the *Talk To* activity to have a face-to-face discussion with one staff member; the *Print* activity to distribute written materials to as many as five staff members; or the *Local Mass Media* activity to influence those who pay attention to the mass media. Each activity requires from one to six weeks to complete, and the player has two academic years (72 weeks) to persuade as many staff members as possible to move through the stages of the innovation-decision process and adopt peer tutoring. The DSG is designed to reward selection of diffusion activities that are appropriate based on DOI theory.

The DSG was originally designed as a board game. In 2002, Frick supervised a development team in the creation of the DSG as an online simulation game (Frick et al., 2003) using HTML, CSS, and XML for information display and storage, and PHP for interaction programming. For a more detailed description of the game, see the design case by Lara et al. (2010). The current version of the game is available at https://diffusion.iu.edu/.

Applying the APT Procedure to the DSG

We modified a copy of the DSG to automatically play games using a strategy-selection algorithm based on DOI theory. Following the APT procedure described above, we first formulated DOI theory as temporal events based on our reading of Rogers (2003). For example, Rogers says that mass media communication channels should be effective in spreading knowledge about an innovation, especially among innovators and early adopters. We then mapped those events to actions that may be taken in the DSG, identified the data associated with those actions, and designed a database for data collection in which the columns are event classifications (e.g., activity selected, current stage in the innovation-decision process for each staff member) and the rows contain the relevant categories in each classification for each turn in a game (see Map 6.1).

84 APT for Evaluation of a Learning Design

Map 6.1 Temporal Map of the First 12 Turns in a Game

recID	step	activity	wTot	tScore	scoreTot	adopters	stScore	Ascore	Aphase
1227	1	personal	1	0	0	0	6	0	
1227	2	personal	2	0	0	0	6	0	
1227	3	personal	3	0	0	0	6	0	
1227	4	personal	4	0	0	0	6	0	
1227	5	personal	5	0	0	0	6	0	
1227	6	talk to	6	3	3	0	6	0	
1227	7	talk to	7	3	6	0	6	1	aware
1227	8	talk to	8	1	7	0	6	0	aware
1227	9	present	11	7	14	0	2.25	0	aware
1227	10	media	12	0	14	0	3.71	2	interest
1227	11	media	13	13	27	0	3.71	0	interest
1227	12	present	16	0	27	0	4.17	0	interest

Note: Each row is one turn in a game. Additional columns (not shown) track each of the game's 23 staff members' progress from awareness to adoption as well as the calculated score for each of the nine strategies described below.

We specified nine strategies that should lead to success in the DSG if the computational model is consistent with the conceptual model (DOI theory). Each of these strategies consisted of a pattern of joint occurrences of categories within the various classifications. To continue the previous example, a turn in the game should be successful if the [classification: *activity*] is [category: *Local Mass Media*] and the majority of staff members who are [classification: *adopter type*] either [category: *innovator*] or [category: *early adopter*] and are in the [classification: *innovation-decision stage*] of either [category: *awareness*] or [category: *interest*]. The nine strategies based on DOI theory are:

1. Target earlier adopters and opinion leaders early in the game to work toward critical mass.
2. Use *Personal Information* and *Talk To* activities to get to know potential adopters.
3. Use *Local Mass Media* and *Print* activities to gain points in the *Awareness* and *Interest* stages among earlier adopters.
4. Use the *Presentation* activity to gain points in the *Awareness* and *Interest* stages.
5. Use the *Demonstration* activity, especially by an opinion leader, to gain points in the *Interest* stage for other potential adopters.
6. Use the *Site Visit* activity to gain points in the *Interest* stage and move into the *Trial* stage.
7. Use the *Pilot Test* activity to gain additional points for those with some points in the *Interest* stage or in the *Trial* stage.

8. Target highly connected individuals to gain additional points in the *Interest* stage among later adopters in their social networks and move them into the *Trial* stage.
9. Use the *Training Workshop (Self)* and *Materials Workshop* activities to gain points in the *Trial* stage.

For a detailed explanation of the rationale behind each strategy, see Myers (2012). We sought confirmation of these associations through expert review, which is sometimes referred to as face validity (Garson, 2009) or psychological validity (Kuppers & Lenhard, 2005; Peters et al., 1998), by searching the relevant literature to identify and then survey scholars who are knowledgeable about DOI theory.

For each strategy described above, we wrote a formula to calculate a score based on the appropriateness of the strategy for each turn in a game. For example, for the *Local Mass Media* activity (Strategy 3), the score is the number of staff members who are *Innovators* or *Early Adopters* and are currently in the *Awareness* or *Interest* stage divided by the total number of *Innovators* or *Early Adopters*. This score is relatively large near the beginning of a game, but it progressively decreases as more staff members move into the *Trial* stage later in the game. Strategy 1 and Strategy 8 are not associated with particular activities but instead prescribe general strategies that pertain to desirable characteristics of certain staff members. Therefore, the scores for these strategies are added to the activity-specific strategies so that the strategy-selection algorithm is optimized to target these influential people.

We spent several weeks writing, debugging, and refining the strategy-selection algorithm until we obtained satisfactory results. Generally, this involved running the program with execution tracing to play from 5 to 20 games and examining the results. This verification method also enabled us to test the original DSG code for errors, of which we found several. We periodically used desk checking to review our code for consistency and to update the documentation of the code. To further reduce the chance of programming errors, we separately wrote formulas in Microsoft Excel to calculate the strategy scores and then imported the game data to compare with the PHP calculations. When we found discrepancies between the strategy-selection algorithm and Excel score calculations, we tracked down the cause and corrected the code.

In summary, our program examines APT classifications and categories relevant to the game state for each turn, calculates a score for each DOI strategy, and selects the highest scoring strategy for that turn. Our hypothesis is that if the DSG accurately represents DOI theory, the majority of games using optimal strategies will be in the highest quartile for points scored.

Data Analysis and Results

The DSG gives players 72 weeks to obtain 22 adopters. The time it takes to implement an activity ranges from one to six weeks. The number of points necessary to turn a particular staff member into an adopter depends largely on his or her adopter type, with *Innovators* requiring as few as 5 points and *Laggards* as many as 14 points. The points are distributed across the *Awareness*, *Interest*, and *Trial* stages that lead to *Adoption*. Obtaining all 22 adopters requires 220 points (although this includes 5 points each for two gatekeepers, the Secretary and the Janitor, neither of whom can become an adopter). When measuring success in the DSG, the number of points obtained is arguably a better metric than the number of adopters obtained. To understand this, imagine a game in which the player obtained eight adopters while the rest of the staff members were still in the *Awareness* or *Interest* stages. Compare this with a game in which the player obtained only five adopters while the rest of the staff members had moved through *Awareness* and *Interest* and were in the *Trial* stage. Overall, the latter player gained many more points toward adoption even though fewer adopters were obtained.

The APT method for model verification prescribes specifying a threshold of confidence (step 5) for determining the accuracy of a computational model. The feedback at the end of a game states that achieving 11 or more adopters is above average performance. The DSG was designed with a major objective of promoting recognition that "innovation diffusion is a complex, difficult, time consuming, and frustrating process (since even well-planned campaigns may result in less than total acceptance)" (Molenda & Rice, 1976, p. 461). In a pilot study of historical gameplay data (Enfield et al., 2012), the mean number of adopters was 13.08 ($n = 2,361$) and the mean number of adoption points was 164.25. However, these figures may have been inflated by programming errors that were later discovered. Given the stochastic nature of situational simulations, along with the purposeful difficulty of the DSG, the definition of success in the game for model verification purposes should be reasonably broad. If we divide the total possible adoption points into quartiles and project a negatively skewed distribution, we might expect the majority of games that use optimal strategies to obtain at least 166 points and no games to score fewer than 110 points. Just how many games should fall into the third and fourth quartiles depends on the designers' goals, which in the case of the DSG include striking a balance between rewarding good choices and conveying the difficulty of change agentry. Designers using the APT method for model verification should decide the desired distribution of scores given optimal strategies before undertaking formative evaluation. Table 6.1 shows Myers' (2012) estimate of a desirable outcome given his understanding of the goals of the DSG.

APT for Evaluation of a Learning Design 87

Table 6.1 Projected Distribution of Games by Number of Adoption Points Obtained

	Adoption Points			
	0–55 pts.	56–110 pts.	111–165 pts.	166–220 pts.
Verification Targets	0%	0%	< 40%	> 60%

Table 6.2 First Dataset: Distribution of Games by Number of Adoption Points

	Adoption Points			
	0–55 pts.	56–110 pts.	111–165 pts.	166–220 pts.
Verification Targets	0%	0%	< 40%	> 60%
First Dataset	0%	1%	82%	17%

We began testing by running the strategy-selection program to play 100 games to check for obvious anomalies. The results were reasonable although we were surprised that no games resulted in 220 points. We decided to examine these data in more detail, because as simulation designers conducting formative evaluation, our next step would be to look for unusual results such as low point scores for strategies. But first we checked the distribution of adoption points to determine whether the threshold for model verification was met (Table 6.2). The majority of games (82 percent) fell into the third quartile, while only 17 percent fell into the fourth quartile.

These results suggested to us that some DOI strategies were not being as effective as predicted and hence the computational model could be improved. Because most of the strategies are associated with particular activities, we decided to examine the number of points being awarded for each activity (Table 6.3).

We were not surprised to find that *Talk To* was the most frequently used activity nor that it had one of the lowest mean scores per turn. It is designed to achieve points mostly in the *Awareness* stage, and in some cases (e.g., when *Laggards* are targeted) no points are scored, but according to the feedback text their antagonism toward the innovation has been diffused. For the *Demonstration* activity, the high frequency of use (12 percent of all turns) combined with a relatively low mean score (3.5 points per turn) warranted further examination. The low mean scores for the *Print* and *Pilot Test* activities and the high mean score for the *Materials Workshop* activity also warranted investigation.

The high use of *Demonstration* was the result of a discrepancy between the DSG designers' understanding and instantiation of DOI theory and Myers'. DOI theory states that once potential adopters are aware of the innovation, a

Table 6.3 First Dataset: Frequency and Scores of Activities for 100 Games

Activity	Turns		
	n	%	M Points
Personal Information	500	14.8	0.0
Talk To	1,153	34.1	1.8
Local Mass Media	176	5.2	8.4
Print	171	5.1	2.4
Presentation	185	5.5	11.0
Demonstration	404	12.0	3.5
Site Visit	78	2.3	8.3
Pilot Test	139	4.1	0.3
Training Workshop (Self)	299	8.8	8.0
Materials Workshop	274	8.1	16.0
Grand Total	3,379	100.0	4.4

demonstration by an opinion leader will likely increase their interest. In our code, we required staff members to have completed the *Awareness* phase, but the original DSG code additionally required that they have at least one point in the *Interest* phase. We experimented and found that modifying the game to use our approach resulted in 85 percent of games in the fourth quartile, which we deemed too high and thus easier than the DSG designers intended.

In investigating the low mean score for *Pilot Test*, we discovered that a staff member who our algorithm selected frequently for this activity was scoring poorly. We found that the staff member, whose adopter type is *Early Majority* and who is an opinion leader and therefore should influence others to move closer to adoption, was grouped with mostly *Late Majority* adopter types, resulting in far fewer points being awarded than expected. We contacted one of the original designers of the DSG, Dr. Michael Molenda, and he agreed that the staff member seemed out of place in that group (personal communication, March 7, 2012).

After addressing the scoring anomalies, a final run of 500 games (Table 6.4) found no significant difference in the mean number of turns per game between the first dataset and this third dataset, $t_{.05}(598) = 0.735$, $p = 0.463$, which was expected. However, there was a significant difference in mean total points, $t_{.05}(598) = 10.839$, $p < 0.000$, and in mean total adopters, $t_{.05}(598) = 7.252$, $p < 0.000$, both of which indicated that the modifications to the game described above improved game scores when optimal strategies were used.

Furthermore, the results were very close to satisfying the threshold for model verification that was specified at the beginning of analysis, with the percentage of games in the fourth quartile exceeding the 60 percent target (Table 6.5).

Table 6.4 Comparison of Descriptive Statistics for Games

Variable	First Dataset (n=100)				Third Dataset (n=500)			
	Mean	SD	Min	Max	Mean	SD	Min	Max
Turns	33.79	2.59	28	40	34.01	2.76	28	44
Total Points	148.74	17.51	96	187	170.72	18.70	103	220
Total Adopters	14.67	2.28	10	19	16.54	2.37	6	22

Table 6.5 Third Dataset: Distribution of Games by Number of Adoption Points

	Adoption Points			
	0–55 pts.	56–110 pts.	111–165 pts.	166–220 pts.
Verification Targets	0%	0%	< 40%	> 60%
Third Dataset	0%	0.4%	38.6%	61.0%

Conclusion

When a simulation or simulation game is designed for educational purposes, the designers must ensure that they achieve the appropriate degree of fidelity with respect to the conceptual model on which it is based. Otherwise, the learning experience may lead to misconceptions based on incorrect feedback. Model verification is a procedure for ensuring that the conceptual model of a real-world phenomenon has been translated into a computational model with sufficient accuracy. The purpose of this study was to test whether APT could be used for the verification of a simulation's computational model to provide quantified evidence of a model's performance.

The APT method of simulation model verification is based on a concept that is easy to understand: pattern matching. Simulation modeling begins by selecting or creating a conceptual model of a system, process, entity, or other phenomenon of interest. If this conceptual model can be used to predict outcomes based on joint and/or sequential patterns of the model's components, it is likely that APT can be used to verify the related computational model by calculating the occurrence of those predicted outcomes in the simulation given the same patterns. Outcomes for highly deterministic models are reliably predictable and should require a high threshold of confidence for verification, while more stochastic models should have a lower threshold to accommodate the variability of outcomes.

The computational model of the DSG initially failed to achieve the desired threshold of confidence for verification. Examination of APT data revealed aspects of the model that were not performing as expected. We made several modifications to the model based on examination of discrepancies in the data and tested the results. These small changes were enough to affect game outcomes so that the threshold of confidence was met, demonstrating that APT provides designers with a methodological approach for testing a computational model, obtaining quantified evidence of its performance, and evaluating the degree to which changes to the model affect outcomes.

We have not incorporated Google Analytics into the DSG at this time. We do, however, keep our own records at IU. We know that from 2014 through 2020, we have had over 18,000 people register for the DSG (a process similar to IPTAT registrations, except we do not ask for their names or other information). We also store turn-by-turn logs of gameplay on our IU webserver. We know that most users play the DSG a number of times, since it is challenging to obtain many adopters. These logs can be turned into temporal maps, similar to what we illustrated in Map 6.1. Myers and Frick (2015) have provided further details on temporal maps for DSG gameplay, APT queries, as well as how the effectiveness of the DSG can be summatively evaluated with APT.

Our goal in Chapter 6 has been to illustrate the value of APT for *formative* evaluation in order to improve the fidelity of the online DSG. Also noteworthy is that these changes were immediately implemented, following the Myers (2012) discoveries through use of APT for simulation model verification. Tens of thousands of DSG players have since benefited from the improved fidelity.

Next, in Chapter 7, we show how APT can be used for *summative* evaluation of instruction when online tracking data are *not* available, as we have as we have described for IPTAT and DSG.

References

Alessi, S. (2000). Simulation design for training and assessment. In H. F. O'Neil & D. H. Andrews (Eds.), *Aircrew training and assessment* (pp. 197–222). Lawrence Erlbaum Associates.

Alessi, S., & Trollip, S. (2001). *Multimedia for learning: Methods and development* (3rd ed.). Allyn and Bacon.

Andrews, D. H., Carroll, L. A., & Bell, H. H. (1995). The future of selective fidelity in training devices. *Educational Technology*, *35*(6), 32–36.

Axelrod, R. (2007). Advancing the art of simulation in the social sciences. In J. P. Rennard (Ed.), *Handbook of research on nature inspired computing for economics and management* (pp. 90–100). Idea Group Reference.

Balci, O. (1997). Verification, validation, and accreditation of simulation models. In S. Andradottir, K. J. Healy, D. H. Withers, & B. L. Nelson (Eds.), *Proceedings of the 1997 Winter Simulation Conference* (pp. 135–141). http://www.informs-sim.org/wsc97papers/0135.PDF

David, N. (2009). Validation and verification in social simulation: Patterns and clarification of terminology. In F. Squazzoni (Ed.), *Epistemological aspects of computer simulation in the social sciences* (pp. 117–129). Springer.

Diffusion Simulation Game (Online Version 1). (2002). Bloomington, IN: Indiana University Press. https://diffusion.iu.edu/

Edelson, D. C., & Reiser, B. J. (2006). Making authentic practices accessible to learners: Design challenges and strategies. In R. K. Sawyer (Ed.), *The Cambridge handbook of the learning sciences* (pp. 193–205). Cambridge University Press.

Enfield, J., Myers, R. D., Lara, M., & Frick, T. W. (2012). Innovation diffusion: Assessment of strategies within the DIFFUSION SIMULATION GAME. *Simulation & Gaming, 43*(2), 188–214. https://doi.org/10.1177/1046878111408024

FAS (Federation of American Scientists). (2006). R&D challenges in games for learning.

Feinstein, A. H., & Cannon, H. M. (2002). Constructs of simulation evaluation. *Simulation & Gaming, 33*(4), 425–440. https://doi.org/10.1177%2F1046878102238606

Frick, T. W. (1990). Analysis of patterns in time (APT): A method of recording and quantifying temporal relations in education. *American Educational Research Journal, 27*(1), 180–204. https://doi.org/10.3102%2F00028312027001180

Frick, T. W., Kim, K.-J., Ludwig, B., & Huang, R. (2003). *A web simulation on educational change: Challenges and solutions for development* [Paper presentation]. The Annual Convention of the Association for Educational Communication and Technology, Anaheim, CA, United States. https://tedfrick.sitehost.iu.edu/aect2003/frick_kim_ludwig_huang.pdf

Garson, G. D. (2009). Computerized simulation in the social sciences. *Simulation & Gaming, 40*(2), 267–279. https://doi.org/10.1177%2F1046878108322225

Gibbons, A. S., McConkie, M., Seo, K. K., & Wiley, D. A. (2009). Simulation approach to instruction. In C. M. Reigeluth & A. A. Carr-Chellman (Eds.), *Instructional-design theories and models: Vol. III: Building a common knowledge base* (pp. 167–193). Routledge.

Gilbert, N. (2004). Computer simulation. In A. Kuper & J. Kuper (Eds.), *The social science encyclopedia* (3rd ed., pp. 145–147). Routledge.

Huang, W. D., & Johnson, T. (2009). Instructional game design using cognitive load theory. In R. E. Ferdig (Ed.), *Handbook of research on effective gaming in education* (Vol. 3, pp. 1143–1165). Information Science Reference.

Kuppers, G., & Lenhard, J. (2005). Validation of simulation: Patterns in the social and natural sciences. *Journal of Artificial Societies and Social Simulation, 8*(4). http://jasss.soc.surrey.ac.uk/8/4/3.html

Lara, M., Myers, R., Frick, T., Karabacak, S., & Michaelidou, T. (2010). A design case: Creating an enhanced version of the Diffusion Simulation Game. *International Journal of Designs for Learning, 1*(1). https://doi.org/10.14434/ijdl.v1i1.867

Liu, D., Blickensderfer, E. L., Macchiarella, N. D., & Vincenzi, D. A. (2009). Simulation fidelity. In D. A. Vincenzi, J. A. Wise, M. Mouloua, & P. A. Hancock (Eds.), *Human factors in simulation and training* (pp. 61–73). CRC Press.

Maier, F. H., & Grossler, A. (2000). What are we talking about: A taxonomy of computer simulations to support learning. *System Dynamics Review, 6*(2), 135–148. https://doi.org/10.1002/1099-1727(200022)16:2%3C135::AID-SDR193%3E3.0.CO;2-P

Molenda, M., & Rice, J. M. (1979). Simulation review: The Diffusion Simulation Game. *Simulation & Games, 10*(4), 459–467. https://doi.org/10.1177%2F104687817901000407

Myers, R. D. (2012). *Analyzing interaction patterns to verify a simulation/game model* (Order No. 3544908) [Doctoral dissertation]. Indiana University. ProQuest Dissertations and Theses Global.

Myers, R. D., & Frick, T. W. (2015). Using pattern matching to assess gameplay. In C. S. Loh, Y. Sheng, & D. Ifenthaler (Eds.), *Serious games analytics: Methodologies for performance measurement, assessment, and improvement* (Chapter 19, pp. 435–458). Springer. https://doi.org/10.1007/978-3-319-05834-4_19

Pace, D. K. (2004). Modeling and simulation verification and validation challenges. *Johns Hopkins APL Technical Digest, 25*(2), 163–172. http://www.jhuapl.edu/Content/techdigest/pdf/V25-N02/25-02-Pace.pdf

Peters, V., Vissers, G., & Heijne, G. (1998). The validity of games. *Simulation & Gaming, 29*(1), 20–30. https://doi.org/10.1177%2F1046878198291003

Reigeluth, C. M., & Schwartz, E. (1989). An instructional theory for the design of computer-based simulations. *Journal of Computer-Based Instruction, 16*(1), 1–10.

Rogers, E. M. (1962). *Diffusion of innovations*. Free Press of Glencoe.

Rogers, E. M. (2003). *Diffusion of innovations* (5th ed.). Simon & Schuster.

Sargent, R. G. (2010). Verification and validation of simulation models. In B. Johansson, S. Jain, J. Montoya-Torres, J. Hugan, & E. Yücesan (Eds.), *Proceedings of the 2010 Winter simulation Conference* (pp. 166–183). Institute of Electrical and Electronic Engineers.

Shaffer, D. W., Squire, K. R., Halverson, R., & Gee, J. P. (2005). Video games and the future of learning. *Phi Delta Kappan, 87*(2), 104–111. https://doi.org/10.1177%2F003172170508700205

Smith, J. E. (1996). Computer simulation. In A. Kuper & J. Kuper (Eds.), *The social science encyclopedia* (2nd ed., pp. 118–120). Routledge.

Thacker, B. H., Doebling, S. W., Hemez, F. M., Anderson, M. C., Pepin, J. E., & Rodriguez, E. A. (2004). *Concepts of model verification and validation* (No. LA-14167-MS). Los Alamos National Laboratory. https://doi.org/10.2172/835920

Whitner, R. B., & Balci, O. (1989). Guidelines for selecting and using simulation model verification techniques. In E. E. MacNair, K. J. Musselman, & P. Heidelberger (Eds.), *WSC'89: Proceedings of the 21st conference on Winter simulation* (pp. 559–568). Association for Computing Machinery. https://doi.org/10.1145/76738.76811

Wideman, H. H., Owston, R. D., Brown, C., Kushniruk, A., Ho, F., & Pitts, K. C. (2007). Unpacking the potential of educational gaming: A new tool for gaming research. *Simulation & Gaming, 38*(1), 10–30. https://doi.org/10.1177%2F1046878106297650

7 Analysis of Patterns in Time with Teaching and Learning Quality Surveys

Summary: We describe an alternative way to determine instructional effectiveness that can be used in a wide range of learning environments—for both online and in-person instruction. The alternative is to have students complete an evaluation instrument called the Teaching and Learning Quality (TALQ) Scales. Students rate their instruction and learning experiences without knowing what First Principles of Instruction are. They rate their experiences by responding to a random mix of Likert-type items. They also rate their own academic learning time (ALT, which is successful engagement), learning progress, satisfaction with the course and instructor, and overall quality of their experience. We provide examples from several studies of how TALQ was used with APT methods to determine effectiveness of FPI and ALT. The advantage of TALQ is that if it is used appropriately, teachers and researchers can determine instructional effectiveness without the technical knowledge and skills required for building websites such as IPTAT.

APT of Course Evaluations

In this chapter we illustrate how Analysis of Patterns in Time (APT) was used in surveys of teaching and learning quality (TALQ). The context for several TALQ studies was through course evaluations in higher education, which were normally administered at or near the end of courses. The evaluations were largely done for in-person courses, though some were done for online courses as well.

Most importantly, *none* of these studies was able to track student behavior during instruction as we were able to do in our Big Study of the online Indiana University Plagiarism Tutorials and Tests (IPTAT), as described in Chapters 2, 3, and 4. We could not easily form temporal maps as was done for IPTAT.

Nonetheless, we were able to do a variation of APT with aggregate data from student course evaluations. In one of the studies (Frick et al., 2010b),

DOI: 10.4324/9781003176343-07

course evaluations were done on paper-and-pencil forms. In the other studies, course evaluations were surveys administered through the Web, where student responses on the surveys were stored digitally with no paper forms involved (Dagli, 2017; Frick et al., 2009; Frick et al., 2010a; and Frick & Dagli, 2016).

We illustrate in this chapter how you can do APT via paper-and-pencil forms, transfer those data to a spreadsheet, and then create formulas to derive APT results. If you can access online survey software or are able to create your own, this will eliminate the time spent on hand-entry of survey results into the spreadsheet. Either way, you should then be able to do the remainder of APT with a spreadsheet or statistical program such as Microsoft Excel, Apple Numbers, Google Sheets, or IBM SPSS (Statistical Product and Service Solutions).

The Goal: Creating a Table from a Spreadsheet

Let's start with the endpoint by providing an example of APT results. Frick et al. (2010b) used APT to analyze relationships among scales derived from a course evaluation instrument on Teaching and Learning Quality (TALQ). In this study, 464 college students completed the TALQ instrument in 12 university classes in business, philosophy, history, kinesiology, social work, informatics, nursing, and health, physical education, and recreation. In this TALQ study there was just one set of measures for each case. In Table 7.1, results are shown for frequencies and percentages of patterns in college classrooms.

Table 7.1 Data from Frick et al. (2010b) Study Used to Do Analysis of Patterns in Time

Student Mastery Level	Agreement on First Principles of Instruction (FPI)							
	No				Yes			
	Agreement on Successful Engagement (ALT)				Agreement on Successful Engagement (ALT)			
	No		Yes		No		Yes	
	Count	%	Count	%	Count	%	Count	%
High (8.5–10)	3	6.4	5	27.8	1	2.3	34	23.0
Medium (6–8)	29	61.7	12	66.7	41	95.3	112	75.7
Low (0–5)	15	31.9	1	5.6	1	2.3	2	1.4
Total	47	100.0	18	100.0	43	100.0	148	100.0

For example, it can be seen from the APT query, "If Agreement on FPI is No and if Agreement on ALT is No, then Student Mastery Level is Low?", this pattern occurred in 15 out of 47 cases, for a probability estimate of 0.319. On the other hand, for the query, "If Agreement on FPI is Yes and if Agreement on ALT is Yes, then Student Mastery Level is Low?", this pattern occurred in just 2 out of 148 cases, for a probability estimate of 0.014. Thus, it can be seen that when students did *not* agree that FPI occurred in their classes *nor* were they successfully engaged, then the likelihood of being rated as a low master by their instructor is much greater than when students *did* agree that FPI and ALT had occurred. The ratio of these probabilities, 0.319 divided by 0.014, is 22.8. Thus, students in this study were about 23 times more likely to be rated at a low mastery level of course objectives when FPI and ALT were perceived to be largely absent in a course, compared with when both were present. Similarly, students were about 3.6 times more likely to be rated as high masters, when both FPI and ALT were present compared with their absence (0.230/0.064), according to student ratings on TALQ scales (Frick et al., 2010b). Note that these results were based on 256 cases in which *independent* instructor ratings of a student's mastery of course objectives matched the student's *independent* self-rating of their mastery.

This is different from the IPTAT analysis in two ways. The TALQ results were derived from:

- Student *perceptions* of their learning experiences after the fact, rather than real-time temporal tracking their learning behavior and experience of instruction designed with First Principles as we did with IPTAT and Google Analytics;
- A single temporal map for each student which represents the *joint occurrence* of *perceived events*, rather than a sequence of events that were tracked within multiple temporal maps for each student.

What is common between the two approaches for doing APT is that we were interested in patterns of learning associated with FPI and student learning achievement. The ways in which we assessed FPI were different, but the overall goal was the same: to evaluate the effectiveness of FPI.

How did we do this?

Formation of TALQ Scales

The history of the development of TALQ is covered in studies by Frick et al. (2009, 2010a, 2010b, 2011). When we redesigned IPTAT in 2015, we initially modified TALQ so it could be used for evaluating *online* instruction such as IPTAT. We referred to the newer version as MOO-TALQ (Dagli, 2017; Frick & Dagli, 2016), so TALQ could also be used for MOOCs (massive open online courses).

The first five questions in the IPTAT MOO-TALQ asked students about which parts of online instruction they did. The remaining 25 questions were adapted from the original TALQ (Frick et al., 2009, 2010a, 2010b, 2011). Following are items on the MOO-TALQ survey used in the redesigned IPTAT in 2016.

1. How many tutorials did you complete (Basic, Novice, Intermediate, Advanced, Expert)?
2. Did you view the video cases in the tutorials?
3. Did you view the demonstrations (with voiceover screencasts)?
4. Did you do reflections, where you wrote about your own experiences or future situations you expect to encounter?
5. Did you do practice questions (with feedback on each answer)?
6. I was very satisfied with this online instruction.
7. I did not do very well on most of the tasks, practice, tests, and other learning activities.
8. I performed a series of increasingly difficult authentic tasks.
9. Skills were demonstrated and examples were provided on what I was expected to learn.
10. When I made errors doing tasks or answering questions, helpful feedback was provided.
11. I engaged in tasks that subsequently helped me learn ideas or skills that were new and unfamiliar to me.
12. I frequently did very well when doing tasks, practice, tests, and other learning activities.
13. I spent a lot of time doing tasks, practice, and other learning activities.
14. The overall quality of this online instruction was outstanding.
15. Illustrations, graphics, movies, and other media helped me to learn.
16. Examples were provided on what I was expected to learn.
17. I put in a great deal of effort and time.
18. I solved authentic problems or completed authentic tasks.
19. I see how I can apply what I learned to real-life situations.
20. A learning structure was provided that helped me to mentally organize new knowledge and skills.
21. I solved a variety of authentic problems or did tasks that were organized from simple to complex.
22. I am able to publicly demonstrate to others what I learned.
23. Skills I was expected to learn were not demonstrated.
24. I had opportunities to practice or try out what I learned.
25. Overall, I would not recommend this online instruction to others.

26. I am able to reflect on, discuss with others, or defend what I learned.
27. I was able to connect my past experience to new ideas and skills I was learning.
28. I received feedback on what I was trying to learn.
29. Alternative ways were provided for understanding the same ideas or skills.
30. This tutorial was a waste of time.

For items 6 to 30, students responded via a standard Likert scale, indicating their degree of agreement or disagreement with each statement: SA = Strongly Agree = 5; A = Agree = 4; U = Undecided = 3; D = Disagree = 2; SD = Strongly Disagree = 1; NA = Not Applicable = 0.

Note that the Likert items were randomly mixed on the survey instrument, not organized according to the MOO-TALQ scales.

We did not know in 2016 that we could have used Google Analytics (GA) tracking and used GA tools to do APT to evaluate the effectiveness of First Principles of Instruction. Thus, in 2016 we proceeded by asking students their perceptions of their experiences, as we did in earlier TALQ studies, rather than observing their actual use of IPTAT as we were later able to do in the Big Study in 2019–2020.

Transferring MOO-TALQ Survey Responses to a Spreadsheet

Dagli (2017) investigated the effectiveness of FPI using MOO-TALQ, which had been incorporated into IPTAT in 2016. Before taking each IPTAT Certification Test (CT), students were given the option to complete MOO-TALQ. Between January 12 and 31, 2016, there were 36,801 students who registered to take a CT.

Dagli (2017) investigated *only* those students who both took a CT and who chose to complete the optional MOO-TALQ survey on their *first* CT attempt. As a result of this exclusion procedure, responses from 2,016 students were included in his study. Of those there were 1,716 students who took CTs for undergraduate and advanced high school students (UG group); whereas 300 students took Certification Tests for graduate students (GR group).

Eight scales in the MOO-TALQ version were designed for student ratings of:

- Overall quality and satisfaction,
- Task engagement,
- Task success,
- FPI authentic problems,
- FPI activation,

Table 7.2 Construction of MOO-TALQ Scales

Scale	Items[a]	Calculation of Scale Mean
Overall quality & satisfaction	6, 14, 25(r), 30(r)	Arithmetic mean from Likert scale rating for each item: strongly disagree = 1, disagree = 2, undecided = 3, agree = 4, strongly agree = 5. Means were computed *after* recoding items with reversed scales (r).
Task engagement	13, 17	
Task success	7(r), 12	
Authentic problems	18, 21	
Activation	11, 20, 27	
Demonstration	9, 15, 16, 23(r), 29	
Application	10, 24, 28	
Integration	19, 22, 26	

Note: [a] (r) = reverse coded

- FPI demonstration,
- FPI application, and
- FPI integration.

As can be seen Table 7.2, each scale consisted of two to five items. Note that four items were negatively worded on purpose to detect whether students were reading the questions carefully. For example, if a student strongly agreed with both items #7 and also #12, this would indicate inconsistent ratings. Those four negatively worded items in the MOO-TALQ were reverse-coded by computing new variables using SPSS 'recode', by which 5 became 1, 4 became 2, 3 stayed the same, 2 became 4 and 1 became 5. Dagli (2017) then examined each scale for internal consistency, and found them to be acceptably reliable, as were earlier versions of TALQ scales (Frick et al., 2009, 2010a, 2010b, 2011).

The mean scores of each scale were calculated by using their respective items shown in Table 7.2. If the mean of a student's ratings on a FPI scale was greater than 3.5, this was categorized as 'agreement' that they experienced that principle.

Creating Spreadsheet Formulas for Each TALQ Scale

After determining whether or not a student agreed that they experienced each FPI (i.e., Agree = 1 if mean score is greater than 3.5; otherwise Disagree = 0), Dagli (2017) counted the number of agreement and disagreement cases within each student mastery level.

To determine a student's mastery level of the IPTAT learning objective, CT results were converted to a three-point ordinal scale based on the number of correct answers to the randomly selected ten questions on a CT. Those who correctly answered zero to five questions were coded as 'low mastery', those who correctly answered six to eight questions were coded as

Table 7.3 Results for the APT Query for Each First Principle for the GR Group

Student Mastery Level	Agreed that Authentic Problems Occurred		Agreed that Activation Occurred		Agreed that Demonstration Occurred		Agreed that Application Occurred		Agreed that Integration Occurred	
	No	Yes	No	Yes	No	Yes	No	Yes	No	Yes
Low	23	35	14	45	15	44	16	43	17	42
Medium	30	126	19	138	14	143	13	143	18	139
High	9	74	8	76	7	77	8	76	6	78
Total	62	235	41	259	36	264	37	262	41	259

Table 7.4 Results for the APT Query for Each First Principle for the UG Group

Student Mastery Level	Agreed that Authentic Problems Occurred		Agreed that Activation Occurred		Agreed that Demonstration Occurred		Agreed that Application Occurred		Agreed that Integration Occurred	
	No	Yes	No	Yes	No	Yes	No	Yes	No	Yes
Low	187	235	140	290	138	292	120	309	138	292
Medium	277	603	211	677	189	700	150	737	205	684
High	84	308	56	340	46	351	32	364	58	339
Total	548	1146	407	1327	373	1343	302	1410	401	1315

'medium mastery', and those who correctly answered nine or ten questions were coded as 'high mastery'. Note that there were two types of CTs: (a) undergraduate and advanced high school students (UG), and (b) master's and doctoral students (GR), the latter comprised of more difficult questions (see Chapter 3).

Table 7.3 shows the number of agreement and disagreement cases for each FPI for the GR group. For instance, 23 students in the GR group who were Low Masters disagreed that they experienced the authentic problems FPI in the tutorial, while 35 students agreed that they experienced that FPI. Similarly, Table 7.4 demonstrates the number of agreement and disagreement cases for each of the FPIs in the UG group.

Creating Further Derived Scores for Scale Agreement (Yes or No)

As stated above, a single joint temporal event for each case was considered. In other words, there was *one* temporal map for each student, consisting of one *joint* event which is a categorization of joint occurrences. Since the

Dagli (2017) study focused on the relationships between FPI, ALT, and student learning achievement, three classifications were created:

- FPI Agreement Scale,
- ALT Agreement Scale, and
- Student Mastery Level.

In order to classify whether or not a student agreed on the presence of any First Principle, scale scores were formed based on students' responses to the MOO-TALQ survey by calculating the mean scores for each scale for each case. In the calculation of scale means, missing values were excluded in SPSS computations. For example, if a student did not respond to one of the items on a three-item scale, the mean was based on their responses to the remaining two items on that scale. Those students whose ratings were greater than 3.5 on all five FPI scales were categorized as 'agreeing' that they experienced FPI in the IPTAT. Those whose ratings were greater than 3.5 on between one and four FPI scales were categorized as 'partially agreeing'. Those students whose ratings were 3.5 or less on all five FPI scales were categorized as 'disagreeing'.

ALT was subsequently constructed as a single variable, based on values of both 'task engagement' and 'task success' scales on the MOO-TALQ. A student who had a mean rating greater than 3.5 on both 'task success' and 'task engagement' scales was categorized as "agreeing" that they experienced ALT; otherwise, the student was categorized as 'disagreeing'.

In summary, there was only one joint temporal event for each student (case) that was coded by categories, respectively, in three classifications as a joint event occurrence. In this study, joint temporal events were considered regardless of their sequence or duration, which is the main difference between the APT method used in the Dagli (2017) study and APT temporal maps with more than one row of joint events (e.g., Sam's and Melinda's maps in Chapter 2).

Creating a Table for the Combinations of Categories

Since there were two different CTs, the APT analyses were performed on each subgroup (GR and UG).

As shown in Table 7.5, there were 119 out of 300 GR test takers who agreed with having experienced ALT and all FPIs. Given that the antecedent condition was true, the consequent (student mastery is 'High') was true in 35 of the 119 cases, which yielded a probability estimate of 35/119 or 0.294. Thus, 29.4 percent of students who were rated as high masters by a CT reported that they also agreed that they experienced both ALT and FPI when using the IPTAT (derived from their ratings of MOO-TALQ scale items).

Table 7.5 Results for the APT Query for GR Students: If Agree that FPI and ALT Occurred, then Student Mastery is ____?

Student Mastery Level	Agreed that ALT Occurred											
	No						Yes					
	Agreed that FPI Occurred						Agreed that FPI Occurred					
	No		Partially		Yes		No		Partially		Yes	
	n	%	n	%	n	%	n	%	n	%	n	%
Low	12	70.6	10	18.2	11	13.4	0	0.0	7	25.9	19	16.0
Medium	4	23.5	28	50.9	47	57.3	0	0.0	13	48.1	65	54.6
High	1	5.9	17	30.9	24	29.3	0	0.0	7	25.9	35	29.4
Total	17	100.0	55	100.0	82	100.0	0	0.0	27	100.0	119	100.0

Table 7.6 Results for the APT Query for UG Students: If Agree that FPI and ALT Occurred, then Student Mastery is ____?

Student Mastery Level	Agreed that ALT occurred											
	No						Yes					
	Agreed that FPI occurred						Agreed that FPI occurred					
	No		Partially		Yes		No		Partially		Yes	
	n	%	n	%	n	%	n	%	n	%	n	%
Low	76	39.6	141	30.1	93	21.1	1	25.0	17	16.8	102	20.0
Medium	97	50.5	241	51.4	229	52.0	2	50.0	58	57.4	262	51.4
High	19	9.9	87	18.6	118	26.8	1	25.0	26	25.7	146	28.6
Total	192	100.0	469	100.0	440	100.0	4	100.0	101	100.0	510	100.0

Next the pattern was investigated where the antecedent condition was no agreement with having experienced both ALT and FPI and where the consequent was high mastery. For this pattern, the antecedent occurred 17 times, the consequent occurred in 1 of those 17 cases, for a probability estimate of 1/17 = 0.059. Thus, 5.9 percent of students who demonstrated high mastery of the objectives of the IPTAT disagreed that they experienced both ALT and FPI.

This finding can be further interpreted: when students perceived that they experienced both ALT and FPI, they were about five times as likely (0.294/0.059 = 4.98) to be high masters compared with those students who did not agree that they experienced ALT and FPI in the IPTAT tutorials.

For the UG test group, using the same calculation approach, as seen in Table 7.6, the APT analyses indicated that 28.6 percent of students who demonstrated high mastery agreed that they experienced ALT and FPI in IPTAT. Furthermore, 9.9 percent of students who demonstrated high mastery of the objectives of the plagiarism tutorial did not agree that they experienced ALT and FPI. This can be further interpreted: when students agreed that they experienced both ALT and FPI, they were about three times as likely (0.286/0.099 = 2.89) to demonstrate high mastery when compared with not agreeing that they experienced ALT and FPI.

Summary

In the Dagli (2017) study, GR students who agreed that they experienced FPI and ALT were about five times as likely to be high masters, when compared with those who did not agree that they experienced FPI and ALT. UG students who agreed that they experienced FPI and ALT were about three times as likely to be high masters compared with those who did not agree. Not only are these findings similar to those in earlier TALQ studies by Frick et al. (2009, 2010a, 2010b, 2011), they are also consistent with results from the Big Study in 2019–2020.

As described in Chapters 2 and 4, we tracked *actual student behavior* when using IPTAT in the Big Study, whereas in the Dagli (2017) study, students reported in MOO-TALQ about their use of parts of IPTAT and about their perceptions of FPI and ALT. In the Big Study, we directly observed student engagement through Google Analytics tracking methods—we did not *ask* students what they did, as had been done in the earlier TALQ and MOO-TALQ studies. Nonetheless, similar conclusions were reached by different approaches that used APT: Successful students were between three and five times more likely to have experienced FPI, regardless of whether:

- student learning achievement was measured by passing an online IPTAT Certification Test, or it was determined by instructor ratings of individual student mastery of course objectives, or by student self-ratings of their own mastery level; and
- student engagement with instruction was directly observed as it was in IPTAT, or it was determined by asking students about their perceived experiences and engagement with instructional activities.

The consistency of findings among these various empirical studies is not only remarkable, these findings also document the overall effectiveness of First Principles of Instruction:

- with high school and university level students,
- in both online and in-person instructional settings, and
- across a wide range of subject matter being taught.

References

Dagli, C. (2017). *Relationships of first principles of instruction and student mastery: A MOOC on how to recognize plagiarism* [Unpublished doctoral dissertation]. Indiana University Graduate School.

Frick, T. W., Chadha, R., Watson, C., & Wang, Y. (2010a). Theory-based evaluation of instruction: Implications for Improving Student Learning Achievement in Postsecondary Education. In M. Orey, S. Jones, & R. Branch (Eds.), *Educational Media and Technology Yearbook*, (Vol. 35, pp. 57–77). Springer.

Frick, T. W., Chadha, R., Watson, C., Wang, Y., & Green, P. (2009). College student perceptions of teaching and learning quality. *Educational Technology Research and Development*, 57(5), 705–720.

Frick, T. W., Chadha, R., Watson, C., & Zlatkovska, E. (2010b). Improving course evaluations to improve instruction and complex learning in higher education. *Educational Technology Research and Development*, 58(2), 115–136.

Frick, T. W., & Dagli, C. (2016). MOOCs for research: The case of the Indiana University plagiarism tutorial and tests. *Technology, Knowledge, and Learning*, 1–22. https://doi.org/10.1007/s10758-016-9288-6

Frick, T. W., Koh, J., & Chadha, R. (2011). Designing effective online courses with first principles of instruction. In R. Roy (Ed.), *Education technology in changing society* (pp. 22–47). Shipra Publications.

8 Analysis of Patterns in Time as an Alternative to Traditional Approaches

Summary: We review the change in perspective which we have provided in this book. When we focus on temporal patterns, we can predict what leads to successful learning outcomes. By making inductive inferences from APT results, predictable patterns of instructional effectiveness can be identified. We further contrast APT with other existing approaches to learning analytics. We conclude by discussing the value of theory for APT and its further extension to MAPSAT: Map and Analyze Patterns and Structures Across Time.

Making Inductive Inferences with APT

In Chapter 1, we used the Oregon Trail as a metaphor for *learning journeys* in education. We described Analysis of Patterns in Time (APT) as an alternative to traditional quantitative and qualitative approaches to do research. We characterized *quantitative methods* as a state-trait approach, which is analogous to taking snapshots of learning journeys, where things are measured as separate variables which are then further analyzed by linear models approaches (LMA).

On the other hand, *qualitative methods* are a storytelling approach to describing learning journeys (e.g., see Creswell & Creswell, 2018; Creswell & Poth, 2018). Such narratives can lead to appreciation of unique learning journeys. However, lack of generalizability is a limitation of qualitative methods. Just because something is true about a few unique cases does not imply that it would be true about *all* cases.

When the goal of educational research and evaluation is to make generalizations, then methods of sampling become paramount. *Inferential statistics* have been developed for scientific research to estimate the likelihood of errors in making inferences from the sample to the population from which the sample is drawn (e.g., see Kirk, 1999, 2013; Tabachnick & Fidell, 2018). In other words, is the sample *representative* of the larger population of cases? If we draw a conclusion from the sample, how likely is it that we would reach the same conclusion if it were possible to study the entire population of cases?

DOI: 10.4324/9781003176343-08

Steiner (1988) summarized the logic of inductive inferences in quantitative methods:

1. A is true of $b_1, b_2, \ldots b_n$; and
2. $b_1, b_2, \ldots b_n$ are some members of class B;
3. hence, A is true of **all** members of class B.

(p. 91, emphasis added)

Steiner reminds us that "'All' is a quantifier" (p. 18).

On the other hand, qualitative research methods are better suited for creation of knowledge of uniques. As Steiner (1988) noted:

> [Q]ualitative structures, if adequate, allow one to be sensitive to the immediacy of the given, to the uniques. They are pervasive qualities. Uniques cannot be members of classes and so no extension is involved. Each is what it is.
>
> (p. 18)

In Chapter 1, we noted that APT is analogous to making documentary movies about learning journeys. Central to APT is the notion of a *temporal map*. A temporal map is a configuration of joint and sequential event occurrences *during* learning journeys. Each temporal map is unique in the qualitative sense, but the larger goal in APT is to identify patterns that are common to many temporal maps. We can adapt Steiner's statement about the form of inductive inference as follows:

1. The likelihood of temporal pattern A is true of temporal maps $b_1, b_2, \ldots b_n$; and
2. temporal maps $b_1, b_2, \ldots b_n$ are some members of class B temporal maps;
3. hence, the likelihood of temporal pattern A is true of **all** members of class B temporal maps.

Note that the results of APT queries are expressed as *likelihoods* of patterns (or as odds ratios). This is no different in principle than weather forecasters predicting that the chance of rain tomorrow in Bloomington is 80 percent, whereas it is 20 percent in Indianapolis. If the likelihood of pattern A is 0.80 and the likelihood of C is 0.20, this is equivalent to saying temporal pattern A is four times more likely than C (0.80 divided by 0.20).

In inferential statistics, an important assumption is that the sample of cases is *randomly selected*. Random selection is a way to help minimize selection bias that could be introduced when choosing cases to study. For example, in Chapter 1, we compared the example of Lewis and Clark's journey in the early 1800s to a hypothetical one by Bill Gates in 2020. This is a non-random sample of Oregon Trail travelers. These were men who were willing to take risks when younger. Bill Gates is further atypical in that he is a multi-billionaire. Note that in this small sample, women and children were excluded, as well as men, women, and children from other countries outside the United States. Poor people were also excluded. This would be selection bias if Lewis, Clark, and Gates comprised the sample of journeys that are being investigated—that is, if the goal of research is to make an inductive inference from the sample to the entire population of cases that might have been observed.

On the other hand, APT queries about temporal patterns result in *descriptive* statistics. Descriptive statistics characterize the cases investigated (e.g., see Kirk, 1999, 2013; Tabachnick & Fidell, 2018). In Chapters 2 and 4, we provided descriptive statistics about temporal patterns observed in a very large number of cases in our Big Study. We collected tracking data from nearly 1.9 million temporal maps of over 936,000 learning journeys. We further know from Google Analytics and from our own registration survey data that users of the Indiana University Plagiarism Tutorials and Tests (IPTAT) were located in 213 countries and territories worldwide, and the large majority were between 14 and 44 years of age. About 86 percent indicated they were in undergraduate and graduate programs in colleges and universities, and about 94 percent were using IPTAT because it was an assignment by their teacher or school. Thus, our Big Study results were true for *this* sample of big data: those who passed a Certification Test (CT) in 2019 and 2020 were between three and four times more likely to view IPTAT web pages that were designed according to First Principles of Instruction (FPI), when compared with those who had not passed a CT. From this we conclude that FPI is generally effective with this population of student learners. Would this be true for everyone for all time? Not necessarily. Our sample did not include young children, for example. Very few were younger than age 14.

Would our conclusions hold true for similar cases in 2021? We do not know with absolute certainty, but we can predict that similar temporal patterns are *highly likely* for IPTAT users in 2021. We have also seen similar patterns in earlier years, 2016 through 2018. We are not trying to make causal statements or to verify a scientific theory in our Big Study when using APT methodology. We are making future predictions based on past behavior.

As a different example, we can predict with a high degree of certainty that sunrise will follow dawn. It keeps happening every day, and has happened for millennia, at least for those not living near the North or South Poles at certain times of the year. We should not conclude that dawn *causes* sunrise, however. This prediction is not a theoretical one. Theories nonetheless could be brought to bear in order to explain this regular temporal phenomenon, especially from Newtonian physics and optical properties of light. Temporal prediction is not the same as theoretical explanation that applies to universals not bound by time and space.

Next, we discuss more recent fields that include data science, educational data mining, and learning analytics. These newer disciplines still face the same issues for quantitative, qualitative, and APT research methodologies that we have been discussing regarding the sampling of cases, prediction of phenomena in the future, and theoretical explanation.

We then conclude this chapter by discussing the value of theory in guiding research and by describing where APT fits into this larger picture.

Big Data in Education

Historically, educational researchers have dealt with what we now consider relatively small data sets (Daniel, 2019), even in cases of national and international assessment (DeBoer & Breslow, 2019). With the widespread use of hypermediated learning environments and ever-increasing computing power, we are now able to collect and store terabytes of data on learners' interactions with digital materials, with instructors, and with other learners. These massive datasets, commonly referred to as *big data*, require new tools and processes to analyze and understand the valuable information they contain (Daniel, 2019). Fischer et al. (2020) noted that "[a]lthough no single unified definition exists, big data are generally characterized by high volume, velocity, and variety" (p. 131).

Fischer et al. (2020) described three overlapping levels of big data. *Microlevel* data are collected frequently, often with a granularity of seconds between actions, as learners interact with/in learning environments. *Mesolevel* data are collected regularly but less frequently, often in a learning management system (LMS) in the form of assignments, discussions, and quizzes. *Macrolevel* data are infrequently updated and include institutional data such as student demographics and course enrollments.

Researchers have referred to microlevel data, such as data collected as learners interact with the IPTAT (described in Chapter 2), as "an audit trail, an information trail, a solution path, a navigation path, and in an education context, an instructional path" (Myers, 2012, pp. 39–40). The more recent literature in learning analytics has used the terms *trace data* and *clickstream data*. Fischer et al. (2020) argued that these data "are uniquely positioned to provide detailed information on students' temporal and sequential patterns of behaviors based on specific actions students undertake and the system design components students utilize" (pp. 135–136). We briefly discuss the methods researchers use to analyze these data below.

Approaches to Big Data

In recent years, two related approaches to working with big data in education have emerged: educational data mining (EDM) and learning analytics (LA). EDM is "concerned with developing methods for exploring the unique and increasingly large-scale data that come from educational settings and using those methods to better understand students, and the settings which they learn in" (International Educational Data Mining Society, n.d.). The Society for Learning Analytics Research (SoLAR, n.d.) defines LA as "the measurement, collection, analysis and reporting of data about learners and their contexts, for purposes of understanding and optimizing learning and the environments in which it occurs." The differences between EDM and LA are subtle, with EDM characterized as focusing on the technological challenges of developing new algorithms and automating knowledge discovery and LA described as focusing on the application of predictive models and development of tools to support decision-making of instructors and learners (Daniel, 2019; Romero & Ventura, 2020). Ultimately, both are interdisciplinary approaches with related objectives and with research methods from computer science, education, and statistics (Romero & Ventura, 2020).

Methods Used to Analyze Big Data

In their systematic review of the LA literature, Mangaroska and Giannakos (2019) found that the most commonly reported methods were regression, correlation, and cluster analysis. In their updated review of the current state of EDM/LA, Romero and Ventura (2020) listed and provided brief descriptions of the most popular EDM/LA methods, which include: causal mining, clustering, discovery with models, distillation of data for human judgment, knowledge tracing, non-negative matrix factorization, outlier detection, prediction, process mining, recommendation, relationship mining (including sequential pattern mining, correlation mining, and causal data mining), statistics, social network analysis, text mining, and visualization.

Recognizing the limitations of the quantitative and qualitative traditions in the social sciences when dealing with big data, in particular commonly used correlational models, several authors have noted that big data require not only greater computing resources but also alternative empirical methods to process and interpret those data (Daniel, 2019; Fischer et al., 2020; Saint et al., 2020).

In reviewing the literature on the use of LA to study self-regulated learning (SRL), Saint et al. (2020) found that most studies, while recognizing the sequential and temporal nature of SRL, generally used only one methodological approach, usually frequency-based statistical analysis. In their own study, Saint et al. applied four analytic methods: simple frequency analysis, epistemic network analysis, temporal process mining, and stochastic process mining. These methods were used separately to answer two research questions, while they were used in combination for a third question. They found each method useful in its own way, while "[t]he combined analysis provides a richer temporal narrative than any one of the individual analyses and allows us to capture the likely movements of behavioural clusters in time and (digital) space" (Saint et al., 2020, p. 410). Consistent with our own findings (see Chapter 2), they concluded that high achievers were more likely to access instructional materials than low achievers, who simply accessed quiz answers. Similarly, Jovanović et al. (2017) compared low and high performers in a flipped classroom context by comparing learning sequences using agglomerative hierarchical clustering. They found that low performers focused more on summative assessments while high performers engaged evenly with all instructional activities.

Learning Analytics and Instructional Design

Among the current topics of interest in the EDM/LA research community that are particularly relevant to APT are (a) the integration of education theories and learning analytics and (b) the analysis of pedagogical strategies using EDM/LA techniques (Romero & Ventura, 2020). However, numerous researchers have lamented the lack of and need for attention given to the application of LA to the design of learning resources and environments (Gašević et al., 2015; Ifenthaler, 2017; Klein & Hess, 2019; Mangaroska & Giannakos, 2019; Phillips & Ozogul, 2020). We would add that researchers fail to go a step further and consider—if not actually investigate—the possibilities of employing LA to test and refine instructional design *theory*.

In their bibliometric analysis of research on LA and educational technology, Phillips and Ozogul (2020) found that the relevant research formed three clusters, the largest being the prediction of student learning outcomes and the next largest being the use of LA to inform instructional design. Research in the second cluster focused on providing instructors with actionable information about student learning progress and the design of instructional resources. However, Phillips and Ozogul noted that these studies "gave little suggestion as to how this information might be utilized to perform real-time interventions" (p. 883). Because the authors found only one link between this cluster and the first on predicting student achievement, they concluded that these two themes are not well integrated.

Wong et al. (2019) conducted a qualitative review of learning analytics research with respect to the use of educational theories and found that the most frequently investigated were SRL, motivation, and social constructivism, noting that the studies reviewed were largely correlational. Perhaps most interesting, from our perspective, was their suggestion that "learning analytics require theories and principles on instructional design to guide the transformation of the information obtained from the data into useful knowledge for instructional design" (p. 4). Despite their exhortation to employ LA to identify patterns of learner behavior and use this information to improve learning theory, which in turn can inform the design of instructional resources, the chapter does not return to this topic to explain how the studies examined can inform instructional design theory.

Lockyer et al. (2013) use the term *learning design* to describe "the sequence of learning tasks, resources, and supports that a teacher constructs for students over part of, or the entire, academic semester" (pp. 1441–1442). Mangaroska and Giannakos (2019) propose a definition of learning analytics for learning design:

> Usage of learners and educators-produced data to discover behavior patterns that are of core interest to both groups, for the purpose of devising explicit, sharable, and reusable learning designs, practices, resources, and tools, aimed at achieving educational goals in a given learning context.
>
> (pp. 519–520)

Regardless of whether one uses the term *learning design* or *instructional design*, there is recognition that "[t]he next frontier in educational research is a synergistic relationship between instructional design and learning analytics" (Ifenthaler, 2017, p. 202) and that LA should prove valuable in creating and testing instructional designs (Lockyer et al., 2013; Phillips & Ozogul, 2020).

The Value of Theory to Guide Educational Research

Kurt Lewin was known for saying, "Nothing is as practical as a good theory" (Greenwood & Levin, 1998, p. 19). Good theory serves to focus design and research. Without good theory, educational data mining, learning analytics, data science, big data, and Analysis of Patterns in Time do not solve a substantive research problem in and of themselves. Broadly speaking, these are research methods, or ways of answering research questions. By themselves, these methods do not tell us what questions to ask.

Applying these approaches to educational research, development, and evaluation without good theory is analogous to big game hunters closing their eyes and using a shotgun, hoping that they might hit something. They

APT as an Alternative 111

might get lucky once in a while, but the "shotgun" approach is both inefficient and ineffective. Just because we have powerful computers and terabytes of data does not solve the problem. These technologies do not even tell us what data to collect in the first place.

We hope that this book demonstrates the value of good theory. When we redesigned IPTAT in 2015, we used instructional design theory. In particular, we used First Principles of Instruction (Merrill, 2002, 2013). We even named web pages after FPI principles, such as 'task1/activation. html' or 'task5/demonstration.html' (see Chapter 2, Table 2.1). Because we approached instructional design this way, we were able to take advantage of Google Analytics (GA) tracking methods, which record names of web pages viewed by clients. If we had not approached our instructional design this way, we would not have known what to look for when doing APT with GA.

APT is itself grounded in theories (see the Epilogue that follows). Frick (1983, 1990) utilized set theory and probability theory from mathematics, information theory, and general systems theory for characterizing systems dynamics. Retroduction from these theories led to the innovation of a new concept for measuring things, namely temporal maps.

APT *queries* are used for matching and segmenting within temporal maps, in order to count occurrences of temporal patterns. APT queries are fundamentally a combination of Boolean logic from mathematics and set theory, and they are similar to other structured query languages in computer science that are used in analyzing data (e.g., SQL). However, APT queries take on special meaning, where the 'if . . . then . . . then. . .' syntax refers to temporal sequences, not just Boolean logical conditions.

Furthermore, APT extends Markov chain theory in mathematics, allowing for sequences longer than two events, and for multiple classifications each with mutually exclusive and exhaustive categories. APT is empirically consistent with traditional Bayesian reasoning, when there is a one-to-one correspondence between antecedent and consequent events, although APT goes beyond Bayes' theorem when many-to-one event relations occur. Frick (1983) described the differences in these theoretical approaches, as well as the differences between APT assumptions and theoretical assumptions required in standard measurement theory and classical statistical theory.

In short, APT has a solid theoretical foundation in several mathematical theories. Of course, APT predates modern learning analytics and learning sciences by decades. APT was developed in the 1970s, whereas the first SoLAR conference was held in 2011. APT is *innovative* learning analytics in this regard.

Extending APT

We would be remiss without mentioning MAPSAT: Map and Analyze Patterns and Structures Across Time (Frick et al., 2008; Myers & Frick, 2015; https://educology.iu.edu/affectRelation.html). MAPSAT extends APT and includes Analysis of Patterns in Configurations (APC). Digraph theory is foundational for MAPSAT, as well as for Axiomatic Theories of Intentional Systems (ATIS: Thompson, 2006, 2019). APT measures system dynamics, whereas APC measures system *structural* properties. We note that others in learning analytics are exploring structural patterns, such as in epistemic network analysis by Shaffer and Ruis (2017), also grounded in digraph theory from mathematics. Space limitation here prevents us from discussing these further advances. For further examples of APT and MAPSAT, see https://aptfrick.sitehost.iu.edu.

As we have noted (Frick et al., 2008; Myers & Frick, 2015):

- In linear models approaches, we measure things separately and then statistically *relate those measures*.
- In MAPSAT, we *measure the relations*.

This is not a play on words, but a significant change of mindset for doing research and evaluation. Our goal in this book has been to provide a roadmap for you to follow so you can also use Analysis of Patterns in Time when investigating learning journeys in education.

References

Creswell, J. W., & Creswell, J. D. (2018). *Research design: Qualitative, quantitative and mixed methods approaches* (5th ed.). SAGE.

Creswell, J. W., & Poth, C. N. (2018). *Qualitative inquiry and research design: Choosing among five approaches* (4th ed.). SAGE.

Daniel, B. K. (2019). Big data and data science: A critical review of issues for educational research. *British Journal of Educational Technology*, 50(1), 101–113. https://doi.org/10.1111/bjet.12595

DeBoer, J., & Breslow, L. (2019). Big data, small data, and data shepherds. In J. Lester, C. Klein, A. Johri, & H. Rangwala (Eds.), *Learning analytics in higher education: Current innovations, future potential, and practical applications* (pp. 45–68). Routledge.

Fischer, C., Pardos, Z. A., Baker, R. S., Williams, J. J., Smyth, P., Yu, R. . . . Warschauer, M. (2020). Mining big data in education: Affordances and challenges. *Review of Research in Education*, 44, 130–160. https://doi.org/10.3102/0091732X20903304

Frick, T. W. (1983). *Nonmetric temporal path analysis: An alternative to the linear models approach for verification of stochastic educational relations* [Unpublished doctoral dissertation]. Indiana University Graduate School.

Frick, T. W. (1990). Analysis of patterns in time (APT): A method of recording and quantifying temporal relations in education. *American Educational Research Journal, 27*(1), 180–204.

Frick, T. W., Myers, R., Thompson, K., & York, S. (2008). New ways to measure systemic change: Map & Analyze Patterns & Structures Across Time (MAPSAT). Featured research paper presented at the annual conference of the Association for Educational Communications & Technology, Orlando, FL. https://tedfrick.sitehost.iu.edu/aect2003/frick_kim_ludwig_huang.pdf

Gašević, D., Dawson, S., & Siemens, G. (2015). Let's not forget: Learning analytics are about learning. *TechTrends, 59*(1), 64–71. https://doi.org/10.1007/s11528-014-0822-x

Greenwood, D. J., & Levin, M. (1998). *Introduction to action research: Social research for social change*. SAGE.

Ifenthaler, D. (2017). Learning analytics design. In L. Lin & M. Spector (Eds.), *The sciences of learning and instructional design: Constructive articulation between communities* (pp. 202–211). Routledge.

International Educational Data Mining Society. (n.d.). *Educational data mining*. https://educationaldatamining.org/

Jovanović, J., Gašević, D., Dawson, S., Pardo, A., & Mirriahi, N. (2017). Learning analytics to unveil learning strategies in a flipped classroom. *The Internet and Higher Education, 33*, 74–85. http://dx.doi.org/10.1016/j.iheduc.2017.02.001

Kirk, R. E. (1999). *Statistics: An introduction* (4th ed.). Harcourt Brace.

Kirk, R. E. (2013). *Experimental design: Procedures for the behavioral sciences* (4th ed.). SAGE.

Klein, C., & Hess, R. M. (2019). Using learning analytics to improve student learning outcomes assessment: Benefits, constraints, & possibilities. In J. Lester, C. Klein, A. Johri, & H. Rangwala (Eds.), *Learning analytics in higher education: Current innovations, future potential, and practical applications* (pp. 140–159). Routledge.

Lockyer, L., Heathcote, E., & Dawson, S. (2013). Informing pedagogical action: Aligning learning analytics with learning design. *American Behavioral Scientist, 57*(10), 1439–1459. https://doi.org/10.1177/0002764213479367

Mangaroska, K., & Giannakos, M. (2019). Learning analytics for learning design: A systematic literature review of analytics-driven design to enhance learning. *IEEE Transactions on Learning Technologies, 12*(4), 516–534. https://doi.org/10.1109/TLT.2018.2868673

Merrill, M. D. (2002). First principles of instruction. *Educational Technology Research & Development, 50*(3), 43–59.

Merrill, M. D. (2013). *First principles of instruction: Identifying and designing effective, efficient, and engaging instruction*. Pfeiffer.

Myers, R. D. (2012). *Analyzing interaction patterns to verify a simulation/game model* (Order No. 3544908) [Doctoral dissertation]. Indiana University. ProQuest Dissertations and Theses Global.

Myers, R. D., & Frick, T. W. (2015). Using pattern matching to assess gameplay. In C. S. Loh, Y. Sheng, & D. Ifenthaler (Eds.), *Serious games analytics:*

Methodologies for performance measurement, assessment, and improvement (Chapter 19, pp. 435–458). Springer.

Phillips, T., & Ozogul, G. (2020). Learning analytics research in relation to educational technology: Capturing learning analytics contributions with bibliometric analysis. *TechTrends, 64*(6), 878–886. https://doi.org/10.1007/s11528-020-00519-y

Romero, C., & Ventura, S. (2020). Educational data mining and learning analytics: An updated survey. *Wiley Interdisciplinary Reviews: Data Mining and Knowledge Discovery, 10*(3), e1355. https://doi.org/10.1002/widm.1355

Saint, J., Gašević, D., Matcha, W., Ahmad Uzir, N., & Pardo, A. (2020, March). Combining analytic methods to unlock sequential and temporal patterns of self-regulated learning. In C. Rensing & H. Drachsler (Eds.), *Proceedings of the Tenth International Conference on learning analytics & knowledge* (pp. 402–411). ACM. https://doi.org/10.1145/3375462.3375487

Shaffer, D. W., & Ruis, A. R. (2017). Epistemic network analysis: A worked example of theory-based learning analytics. In C. Lang, G. Siemens, A. Wise, & D. Gašević (Eds.), *Handbook of learning analytics* (1st ed., Chapter 15, pp. 175–187). Society of Learning Analytics Research. https://doi.org/10.18608/hla17

Society of Learning Analytics Research. (n.d.). *What is learning analytics?* http://www.solaresearch.org/about/what-is-learning-analytics/

Steiner, E. (1988). *Methodology of theory building*. Educology Research Associates.

Tabachnick, B. G., & Fidell, L. S. (2018). *Using multivariate statistics* (7th ed.). Pearson.

Thompson, K. R. (2006). Axiomatic theories of intentional systems: Methodology of theory construction. *Scientific Inquiry Journal, 7*(1), 13–24.

Thompson, K. R. (2019). Axiomatic theory of intentional systems (ATIS) and options-set analyses for education. In M. Spector, B. Lockee, & M. Childress (Eds.), *Learning, design, and technology*. Springer. https://doi.org/10.1007/978-3-319-17727-4_93-1

Wong, J., Baars, M., de Koning, B. B., van der Zee, T., Davis, D., Khalil, M., & Paas, F. (2019). Educational theories and learning analytics: From data to knowledge. In D. Ifenthaler, D.-K. Mah, & J. Y.-K. Yau (Eds.), *Utilizing learning analytics to support study success* (pp. 3–25). Springer. https://doi.org/10.1007/978-3-319-64792-0_1

Epilogue

Summary: The first author tells the story of the serendipitous discovery of Google Analytics as a way to do Analysis of Patterns in Time. It concludes by describing the 50-year journey that has culminated in this book. Acknowledgments follow.

The Important New Discovery in February 2020 by the First Author

This book has been nearly 50 years in the making. But it is mostly about an important discovery in late February 2020. While I was staying at home as novel coronavirus was emerging in the U.S., I was routinely checking our Indiana University Plagiarism Tutorials and Tests (IPTAT, 2002-present) website using Google Analytics, just to see what web pages had been viewed recently. We have been using Google Analytics since 2016 for tracking use of the IPTAT website; and it has been quite helpful to see how these online tutorials and tests are being used by students from all over the world (Frick & Dagli, 2016; Google Analytics, 2005–present). We also keep our own records at IU on students who register for IPTAT and pass one of the trillions of Certification Tests we provide online.

Late that February evening, I began to explore some features of Google Analytics that I had not probed in any depth before. I had noticed an administrative option to do 'segmenting' in Google Analytics reports. As I began to explore what could be done with Google Analytics segments, I experienced a big "aha!" moment—serendipity happened. It suddenly dawned on me that we might be able to do some variation of Analysis of Patterns in Time (APT) if we could cleverly adapt Google Analytics reporting tools that included segmenting of users and specifying logical expressions for matching names of web pages viewed or other conditions of usage. I first invented APT in the early 1970s (then called NTPA); and my students, colleagues, and I have further developed APT since then, now approaching 50 years.

I spent the next two weeks seeing how far I could push Google Analytics to do APT. Within a month, I had demonstrated, at least to my own satisfaction, that we could use Google Analytics to do APT as a way to determine the effectiveness of First Principles of Instruction, which were used to redesign IPTAT in 2015. What I found from APT was that successful students were about four times more likely overall to choose parts of our online tutorials that were designed with First Principles of Instruction, when compared with unsuccessful students! Success was measured by passing a Certification Test on how to recognize plagiarism.

We have a wealth of data, as it turns out. In the five years since we started with Google Analytics, we've had about 85 million pageviews of IPTAT. In that temporal window beginning in 2016, nearly 750,000 students worldwide from 225 countries and territories have passed one of our Certification Tests on *How to Recognize Plagiarism*. In other words, these APT findings have wide generalizability. *Worldwide* generalizability.

Then I shared my excitement with a few colleagues, including the co-authors. I started documenting what I was doing with Google Analytics to do APT, so they could carry on if something should happen to me. I realized that if I did not survive the COVID pandemic, this important discovery might be lost. I soon found that my documentation and notes were getting too extensive to put into a typical research paper. My goal was to provide a roadmap for others to follow, so they could carry on without me. As my explanations and examples continued to grow, I realized that I was writing a guidebook, which we are now sharing with you, so you too can do APT to help advance knowledge of effective instruction.

Most importantly, we have enormous evidence at our fingertips about the effectiveness of First Principles of Instruction, which we used to redesign IPTAT in 2015. In many places around the world, teachers and students were suddenly thrust into doing more remote teaching and learning, due to the worldwide coronavirus pandemic. Our findings could benefit this unfortunate, but real, situation. Our IPTAT findings could also benefit traditional in-person instruction and learning.

Prior to this discovery, I had been putting off a large software development project to provide tools for researchers to do APT. I understood the enormity of the task, but my heart was not in such a major undertaking at this point in my life. Then it suddenly dawned on me that night in February that talented software engineers at Google had already figured out how to do APT. Their goal is to help business advertisers determine what sequences of user actions on the Web that result in sales, that is, that lead to profits. Google engineers had solved the numerous challenges we were facing with APT software, not the least of which was the necessary infrastructure to collect the data on temporal events, as well as ways of helping their business clients identify what advertisements and other strategies were successful in attracting potential customers.

This is exactly the same research problem APT was designed to address, except that we are interested in what promotes student learning achievement, especially what methods or strategies teachers and instructional designers can use to increase the likelihood of student success.

It Began about 50 Years Ago...

I recall that when I was just starting graduate school in the early 1970s two things struck me as especially puzzling.

1. I read many empirical research studies in education in prominent journals, and I was often disappointed in the lack of results that might improve educational methods. I wondered why there were so many studies that were unable to show connections with teaching methods and student learning achievement. I could not really find any at the time—not in professional research journals in education.
2. I read a small book, entitled, *Do Teachers Make a Difference?* This government report by the United States Bureau of Educational Personnel Development (1970) was a follow-up to the report by Coleman et al. (1966) on equality of educational opportunity in the U.S. The earlier nationwide study had empirically documented that the socioeconomic status (SES) of students and their peers in school was the strongest predictor of student achievement, as measured by standardized tests. Nothing else seemed to matter very much. Coleman et al. (1966) had concluded that "schools bring little influence to bear on a child's achievement that is independent of his [family] background and general social context" (p. 325). The authors of the 1970 publication wondered, was it actually true that teachers do not make a difference, or is there something problematic with multiple regression analysis, the method of research that was employed in the Coleman study? My thoughts were: of course, teachers make a difference; why can't educational researchers document this? What's wrong with this picture?

I was fortunate early on in graduate school to be working on a large-scale empirical study on mainstreaming of mildly disabled students. *Mainstreaming* is now referred to as *inclusion*, but the basic idea is the same. Instead of isolating disabled students in special education classrooms—as was the prevailing practice of the time—students with disabilities could be integrated into regular classrooms with normal students.

This study was referred to as Project PRIME, coordinated by the U.S. Bureau of Education for the Handicapped (BEH) in Washington, DC, the University of Texas in Austin, and Indiana University in Bloomington (Kaufman et al., 1973). The major research question addressed: For whom and under what conditions is mainstreaming of disabled students a viable educational alternative? A further goal of Project PRIME was to provide empirical evidence to inform the U.S. Congress as it was drafting new legislation. Passed in 1975, Public Law 94–142 mandated that all school-age children with disabilities must be provided with a free and appropriate public education (see, for example: https://www2.ed.gov/about/offices/list/osers/idea35/history/index_pg10.html#:~:text=When%20it%20was%20passed%20in,local%20community%20across%20the%20country).

Project PRIME was conducted in 43 school districts throughout the state of Texas, and included thousands of students with disabilities, non-disabled students, special education teachers, and regular classroom teachers in elementary schools. Among the numerous measures used in the study were thousands of hours of classroom observation. Trained observers coded how teachers managed student behavior and misbehavior, student engagement and participation in class, and cognitive demands made by teachers of non-disabled students and those with disabilities. Student achievement was measured by standardized tests, and numerous additional questionnaires were completed by teachers and students themselves, including measures of SES.

For me this was a great learning experience. I was working alongside experts, as an eager and wide-eyed apprentice. I was fortunate to be working with some of the top researchers in the field at the time, including statisticians such as Professor Donald Veldman at the University of Texas, who also wrote software programs for data analysis. Veldman was the author of EDSTAT, a set of widely used FORTRAN programs to do statistical analysis in educational research, which included ANOVA, correlation, multiple regression, factor analysis, and other linear models.

I had great hopes for Project PRIME. I expected that we could empirically show temporal relationships between what was happening in classrooms, what teachers did, and student learning achievement. One of my tasks was training classroom observers and to demonstrate that their data were reliable and trustworthy. As an aside, this task later led to my first major publication in the *Review of Educational Research* (Frick & Semmel, 1978): Observer Agreement and Reliabilities of Classroom Observational Measures. I later co-authored two book chapters on Project PRIME results (Semmel & Frick, 1985a, 1985b).

We ran into a number of problems in how to analyze literally truckloads of paper data for optical scanning, resulting in about 12.7 *miles* of magnetic computer tape (28 large reels) required to store the information digitally (Kaufman et al., 1983, p. 57). Although classroom observational data could have been analyzed temporally for patterns, it was highly impractical with the mainframe computer technology in 1972–73. Classroom observation data on teacher and student variables was aggregated *independently*. Consequently, temporal sequences were irretrievably lost after constructing those independent measures during data reduction. Like Humpty Dumpty after his fall, the particular way in which the pieces of his shell had been connected together could not be reconstructed.

This experience convinced me that there was something fundamentally wrong with approaching multiple regression analysis this way. I was working with some of the best minds in educational research and statistics, and yet we were unable to *temporally connect* what teachers and students did in classrooms with how well those students learned. I was not alone in my frustration. Others with similar experiences with quantitative correlational methods began to look for alternatives. For example, a professor at IU, Egon Guba, was one of the early leaders in developing a movement towards what we now know as qualitative research methods (e.g., Guba & Lincoln, 1981).

About the same time as Project PRIME, I was first exposed to general systems theory in graduate school, especially working with professors George Maccia and Elizabeth Steiner. This had led me to start investigating system processes. I delved deeply into information theory, which was part of the SIGGS Theory Model (Maccia & Maccia, 1966). SIGGS was retroduced from set, information, di-graph, and general systems theories. A further source of influence in my thinking was reading about Collett and Semmel's (1971) work on sequential analysis and Markov chains (in mathematics).

I still recall vividly one winter evening in 1976 after a class at George and Liz's house on educational theory development and the SIGGS model. I was standing at a portable blackboard with George, as I was struggling with the difference between information theory, standard measurement theory, and analysis with statistical linear models. He was explaining to me how information was a mapping of categories, as contrasted with a Cartesian coordinate system in algebra. It was then that the proverbial light went off in my head, a giant "aha" experience.

Over the next several years, this led to early formations of what I began to call nonmetric temporal path analysis (NTPA). This became the focus of my Ph.D. thesis, which took me about eight years to complete. During that interval I co-authored two funded research grants, which helped me further develop these ideas. Very importantly, these grants allowed me time and support for developing a set of computer software programs to carry out NTPA. These apps ran on microcomputers that were emerging at the time (TRS-80 and Apple II). I was convinced that NTPA was a way to show the connections between what teachers and students did and how well students learned. Project CARTLO (Computer-Assisted Research into Teaching-Learning Outcomes) and a subsequent observational study of student academic learning time, student engagement, and success in elementary schools in essence helped fund my dissertation research, since my NTPA development was part of these projects.

I found that I also needed to understand probability theory and inferential statistics from the ground up. A book by Samuel Schmitt (1969), *Measuring Uncertainty*, was very influential in grounding my thinking—as I further learned about Bayesian reasoning, sequential analysis, and decision theory, when contrasted with classical statistical inference with probability density functions such as Beta, Gau, Poisson, etc. I later wrote computer programs to operationalize several of these methods, including the Sequential Probability Ratio Test, and binomial and beta distributions for Bayesian reasoning. I discovered how much better and more deeply I understood the mathematics if I wrote software to carry out the reasoning and estimation processes.

Despite the clear and obvious findings from my research on NTPA (Frick 1983, 1990), it was met with considerable skepticism from the larger educational research community. I had a number of conference proposals rejected, such as to the American Educational Research Association, with comments that labeled my ideas as essentially pie-in-the-sky, implying that I was a novice who didn't know what he was talking about, or that I didn't really understand quantitative methods. But, of course, I did understand quantitative methods very well—I even had modified some of Veldman's FORTRAN programs on factor analysis. I could write software that did the analyses. I even mathematically proved the incompatibility of NTPA and linear models at the heart of how we measure things. I had further showed empirically in my dissertation the stark differences in results between the two approaches to measurement and subsequent analytic procedures. I later received a handwritten letter from Professor Lee Cronbach, a prominent statistician at Stanford University, who advised me to abandon NTPA. He saw it as no different than aptitude-treatment interactions (ATI), which he and Richard Snow had invented to deal with the problem with linear models that we all recognized (Cronbach & Snow, 1977). Cronbach did not understand the difference either between measurement approaches in NTPA vs. linear models.

I recall a conversation with George Maccia, when I confided with him how disheartened I was about the lack of acceptance of NTPA. Since I was highly skilled with computers, he suggested that I build on that background when seeking a faculty position. I had originally planned on joining faculty in an educational psychology program on research methods;

and I had my eye on the University of Virginia at the time. I had been very impressed by Professor Donald Medley's work on classroom observation research when I had met with him in Charlottesville during Project PRIME.

And then an opportunity suddenly emerged for a position in Instructional Systems Technology (IST) at IUB, in late spring 1983. I applied for the faculty position, not expecting to be even considered since I was an IU graduate (or would be, as soon as I had finished my dissertation!). As it turned out, I did get hired as a new faculty member in IST. The position was created in order to develop the then non-existent computer curriculum in IST course offerings. I also recall George's advice—work towards tenure by doing research on computers in education, which was in great demand, since desktop computers were just coming out at the time. Put NTPA on the back burner until after you get tenure. And keep doing more studies that show the value of this approach.

I did follow George's advice, and much of the rest of this story can be gleaned from my vita: https://tedfrick.sitehost.iu.edu/vita.html. As it turned out, I got waylaid by the emergence of the Web in the early 1990s. The World Wide Web was just too important to ignore, since I could see that it, coupled with personal computers, would change everything—much as had Guttenberg's invention of the printing press 500 years earlier. In the meantime, I continued to teach doctoral students about Analysis of Patterns in Time (APT), a new name I had given to NTPA, when I published the seminal study (Frick, 1990).

Life happened, as they say. Before I knew it, I became the Web Director for the School of Education, leading efforts to build the website. This large SoE website helped to recruit students to our programs by providing useful information about our academic programs, details about our courses, accomplishments of faculty, and prospects for employment after graduating (Frick et al., 2005). After I had stepped down as SoE Web Director, I realized during my 2005 sabbatical that the Web could also be used as a vehicle for doing research.

When I began to form research teams in our newly revised Ph.D. program in Instructional Systems Technology, I knew that we had two existing web applications that we might utilize for doing research studies. Since these apps were used by tens of thousands of students, this would address the typical problem in education research—sample sizes were often too small or unrepresentative of the larger population, limiting generalizability of findings. These two apps were (1) the *Plagiarism Tutorial and Test: How to Recognize Plagiarism*, and (2) the *Diffusion Simulation Game*. I was still interested in promoting APT by example in further studies by doctoral students and co-authored publications in research journals. And away we went.

You can get some idea of the projects by my web page on research teams: https://tedfrick.sitehost.iu.edu/research_groups.html.

I hope that my co-authors will carry on with APT and its further dissemination. APT is after all, an innovation to be adopted, with the expectation that this will help advance praxiological knowledge of education. I hope that this book will facilitate the journey to greater adoption—of not only Analysis of Patterns in Time, but also First Principles of Instruction.

It appears that Google has been the biggest adopter of APT thus far, and so has Major League Baseball. People in these organizations may not know they are doing APT as I envisioned it nearly 50 years ago, but as we have noted in this book, indeed they *have* been doing Analysis of Patterns in Time. We hope that more people in education will see the value of APT and First Principles of Instruction. We have provided a roadmap, so you and others can do this too.

Acknowledgments

Many individuals have contributed either directly or indirectly to the development of APT in past decades, whom I want to acknowledge briefly. They are listed alphabetically by first name.

Professors who were Significant Mentors

- Elizabeth Steiner: who modeled the appreciation of truth, goodness, and beauty, who demonstrated critical thinking and courage to think differently, and who helped me understand educology.
- George Maccia: who helped me see the difference between linear models with algebraic functions and information theoretic mappings—stimulating my initial breakthrough with APT, and who mentored me on epistemology throughout his lifetime.
- Leon Fosha: who helped me realize that I had not abandoned my previous music education, but rather that I had just changed instruments—from playing the clarinet to playing with computers and learning.
- Melvyn Semmel: who piqued my interest in sequential analysis of classroom observations, who provided invaluable research experiences in Project PRIME, and who supported an environment for innovative R&D while I was a doctoral student.
- Michael Orme: who first introduced me to educational research when I was an undergraduate student, who demonstrated that some teaching techniques and strategies were more effective than others, and who taught me that teacher and student classroom behavior could be coded by trained observers as part of educational research studies.

Doctoral Students who Used APT Methods in their Research Studies

- Andrew Barrett
- Cesur Dagli
- Christine Fitzpatrick
- Christopher Hebb
- Craig Howard
- David Ding-Kuo Sze
- Edwin Welch
- Emily Powell
- Hing-Kwan Luk
- Jaesoon An
- Joyce Koh
- Kyungsu Wang
- Miguel Lara
- Rodney Myers
- Roger Yin
- Thomas Plew

Over the decades there were countless other students, colleagues, and critics who asked good questions—who helped sharpen my own thinking about APT—too many to mention specifically.

Finally, I want to give special thanks for important and helpful editorial suggestions for this book by Curtis Bonk, Gena Asher, Judy Brophy, and Kathy Frick.

Ted Frick
March 14, 2021
Bloomington, Indiana, USA

References

Coleman, J. S., Campbell, E. Q., Hobson, C. J., McPartland, J., Mood, A. M., Weinfeld, F. D., & York, R. L. (1966). *Equality of educational opportunity.* Washington, DC: U.S. Government Printing Office. http://www.google.com/books/edition/Equality_of_Educational_Opportunity/TdRf6VHr2RgC?hl=en&gbpv=1&printsec=frontcover

Collett, L. S., & Semmel, M. I. (1971). *The analysis of sequential behavior in classrooms and social environments: Problems and proposed solutions.* Bloomington, IN: Center for Innovation in Teaching the Handicapped, Indiana University.

Cronbach, L. J., & Snow, R. E. (1977). *Aptitudes and instructional methods: A handbook for research on interactions.* Irvington.

Frick, T. W. (1983). *Nonmetric temporal path analysis: An alternative to the linear models approach for verification of stochastic educational relations* [Unpublished doctoral dissertation]. Indiana University Graduate School.

Frick, T. W. (1990). Analysis of patterns in time (APT): A method of recording and quantifying temporal relations in education. *American Educational Research Journal, 27*(1), 180–204.

Frick, T. W., & Dagli, C. (2016). MOOCs for research: The case of the Indiana University plagiarism tutorials and tests. *Technology, Knowledge and Learning, 21*(2), 255–276.

Frick, T. W., & Semmel, M. I. (1978). Observer agreement and reliabilities of classroom observational measures. *Review of Educational Research, 48*(1), 157–184.

Frick, T. W., Su, B., & An, Y.-J. (2005). Building a large, successful website efficiently through inquiry-based design and content management tools. *TechTrends, 49*(4), 20–31.

Google Analytics. (2005-present). Retrieved August 18, 2020, from https://en.wikipedia.org/wiki/Google_Analytics

Guba, E. G., & Lincoln, Y. S. (1981). *Effective evaluation: Improving the usefulness of evaluation results through responsive and naturalistic approaches.* Jossey-Bass.

Indiana University Plagiarism Tutorials and Tests. (2002-present). How to recognize plagiarism. https://plagiarism.iu.edu

Kaufman, M. J., Agard, J. A., & Semmel, M. I. (1985). *Mainstreaming: Learners and their environments.* Brookline Books.

Kaufman, M. J., Semmel, M. I., & Agard, J. A. (1973). *Project PRIME: Interim report, 1971–1972-Purposes and procedures.* Washington, DC: U.S. Office of Education, Bureau of Education for the Handicapped.

Maccia, E. S., & Maccia, G. S. (1966). *Development of educational theory derived from three educational theory models (Project Number 5–0638).* Office of Education, U.S. Department of Health, Education, and Welfare.

Schmitt, S. (1969). *Measuring uncertainty.* Addison-Wesley.

Semmel, M. I., & Frick, T. (1985a). Learner background characteristics. In M. Kaufman, J. A. Agard, & M. I. Semmel (Eds.), *Mainstreaming: Learners and their environments* (pp. 75–98). Brookline Books.

Semmel, M. I., & Frick, T. (1985b). Learner competence in school. In M. Kaufman, J. A. Agard, & M. I. Semmel (Eds.), *Mainstreaming: Learners and their environments* (pp. 99–150). Brookline Books.

United States Bureau of Educational Personnel Development. (1970). *Do teachers make a difference? A report on recent research on pupil achievement* [OE-58042]. U.S. Government Printing Office.

Abbreviations and Symbols

Note: '$=_{df}$' means 'equals by definition'

Abbreviations

A $=_{df}$ Agree (in Likert scale)
ALT $=_{df}$ Academic Learning Time
ANCOVA $=_{df}$ Analysis of Covariance (in statistics)
ANOVA $=_{df}$ Analysis of Variance (in statistics)
APC $=_{df}$ Analysis of Patterns in Configuration (part of MAPSAT)
APT $=_{df}$ Analysis of Patterns in Time: https://aptfrick.sitehost. iu.edu (now part of MAPSAT)
ATI $=_{df}$ Aptitude-Treatment Interaction
ATIS $=_{df}$ Axiomatic Theories of Intentional Systems
BEH $=_{df}$ Bureau of Education for the Handicapped (U.S.)
CARTLO $=_{df}$ Computer-Assisted Research into Teaching-Learning Outcomes
COVID $=_{df}$ Coronavirus Disease
CSS $=_{df}$ Cascading Style Sheets: http://www.w3.org/Style/CSS/Overview.en.html
CT $=_{df}$ Certification Test (part of IPTAT): https://plagiarism.iu.edu/certificationTests/
D $=_{df}$ Disagree (in Likert scale)
DI $=_{df}$ Direct Instruction
DOI $=_{df}$ Diffusion of Innovations
DSG $=_{df}$ Diffusion Simulation Game: https://diffusion.iu.edu
EDM $=_{df}$ Educational Data Mining
EDSTAT $=_{df}$ Educational Statistics package
EN $=_{df}$ Student Engagement

FORTRAN = $_{df}$ programming language in computer software engineering (formula translation): https://en.wikipedia.org/wiki/Fortran

FPI = $_{df}$ First Principles of Instruction

GA = $_{df}$ Google Analytics: https://analytics.google.com

GA4 = $_{df}$ Google Analytics 4 (introduced in October 2020): https://support.google.com/analytics#topic=9143232

GR = $_{df}$ Graduate student group (master's or doctoral level)

HTML = $_{df}$ Hypertext Markup Language: https://en.wikipedia.org/wiki/HTML

IBM = $_{df}$ International Business Machines: http://www.ibm.com

ID = $_{df}$ identification, usually by a unique number

IEDMS = $_{df}$ International Educational Data Mining Society: https://educationaldatamining.org/

If . . . then . . . then. . . = $_{df}$ An APT query for finding matches for chains of event conditions in temporal maps, interpreted to mean that: if certain antecedent event conditions occur, then consequent event conditions occur when all antecedent event conditions still remain true, then further consequent event conditions occur when all antecedent event conditions still remain true in the order specified, etc.). See Frick (1983) for APT query syntax and terminology: https://tedfrick.sitehost.iu.edu/ntpa/ (Chapter 2)

IPTAT = $_{df}$ Indiana University Plagiarism Tutorials and Tests: https://plagiarism.iu.edu

IST = $_{df}$ Instructional Systems Technology

IU = $_{df}$ Indiana University: http://www.iu.edu

IUB = $_{df}$ Indiana University Bloomington: http://www.iub.edu

LA = $_{df}$ Learning Analytics

LMA = $_{df}$ Linear Models Approach

LMS = $_{df}$ Learning Management System

MANOVA = $_{df}$ Multivariate Analysis of Variance (in statistics)

MAPSAT = $_{df}$ Map & Analyze Patterns & Structures Across Time: https://mapsat.iu.edu

Max = $_{df}$ Maximum

Min = $_{df}$ Minimum

MLB = $_{df}$ Major League Baseball (U.S.)

MOO-TALQ = $_{df}$ Massive Open Online Teaching and Learning Quality (survey scales)

MOOC = $_{df}$ Massive Open Online Course

MySQL = $_{df}$ My Structured Query Language: http://www.mysql.com

NA = $_{df}$ Not Applicable

ND = $=_{df}$ Non-Direct Instruction
NE = $=_{df}$ Student Non-Engagement
NTPA = $=_{df}$ Nonmetric Temporal Path Analysis (later renamed APT): https://tedfrick.sitehost.iu.edu/ntpa/
PHP = $=_{df}$ PHP Hypertext Preprocessor (a web programming/scripting language): http://www.php.net
PRIME = $=_{df}$ Programmed Reentry into Mainstreamed Education
SA = $=_{df}$ Strongly Agree (in Likert scale)
SD = $=_{df}$ Standard Deviation (in descriptive statistics)
SD = $=_{df}$ Strongly Disagree (in Likert scale)
SES = $=_{df}$ Socioeconomic Status
Seq# = $=_{df}$ Sequence number (in a temporal map)
SIGGS = $=_{df}$ Set, Information, Graph, and General Systems (theory model)
SoE = $=_{df}$ School of Education at IUB: https://education.indiana.edu
SoLAR = $=_{df}$ Society for Learning Analytics Research: http://www.solaresearch.org
SPSS = $=_{df}$ originally referred to the Statistical Package for the Social Sciences
SPSS = $=_{df}$ Statistical Product and Service Solutions, changed after acquisition by IBM
SQL = $=_{df}$ Structured Query Language
SRL = $=_{df}$ Self-Regulated Learning
TALQ = $=_{df}$ Teaching and Learning Quality (survey scales)
Test ID = $=_{df}$ a unique number to identify a specific CT from trillions of other CTs.
U = $=_{df}$ Undecided (in Likert scale)
UA = $=_{df}$ Universal Analytics (introduced by Google in 2012): https://support.google.com/analytics#topic=10094551
UG = $=_{df}$ Undergraduate level group (student in post-secondary education, usually seeking a bachelor's or associate's Degree)
UITS = $=_{df}$ University Information Technology Services (at Indiana University): https://uits.iu.edu/
U.S. = $=_{df}$ USA = $=_{df}$ United States of America
XML = $=_{df}$ Extensible Markup Language: http://www.w3.org/XML/

Symbols

− = $=_{df}$ subtract (in arithmetic)
... = $=_{df}$ pattern that continues (in lists of things)
× = $=_{df}$ multiplied by (in arithmetic)
∩ = $=_{df}$ conjunction of (in logic or set theory, sometimes symbolized by & or *AND*)

Abbreviations and Symbols

| = $_{df}$given that (in probability theory, set theory, or Bayesian Reasoning)

(r) = $_{df}$reversed scale (in Likert scale: Strongly Agree becomes Strongly Disagree, Agree becomes Disagree, Disagree becomes Agree, Strongly Disagree becomes Strongly Agree)

(x,y) = $_{df}$in set theory, an ordered pair; a data point in a Cartesian Coordinate System (where the x-axis and y-axis coordinates intersect: https://en.wikipedia.org/wiki/Cartesian_coordinate_system)

* = $_{df}$asterisk, often used as a wildcard character which matches one or more characters in computer file names; can also serve as a footnote for written text

/ = $_{df}$forward slash: divided by (in arithmetic, also symbolized as ÷)

% = $_{df}$percent (per one hundred); also can used as a wildcard character which matches one or more characters in computer search strings

† = $_{df}$true (for APT query segment match)

+ = $_{df}$add (in arithmetic)

= = $_{df}$equals (in arithmetic and algebra)

~ = $_{df}$approximately equal (in algebra or arithmetic)

n = $_{df}$number (integer)

ø = $_{df}$false (for APT query segment match)

p = $_{df}$probability (likelihood or proportion)

R = $_{df}$multiple correlation coefficient (in statistics)

r = $_{df}$Pearson Product Moment correlation coefficient for interval and ratio level variables (in statistics)

R^2 = $_{df}$square of multiple correlation coefficient (which estimates the percent of variance accounted for in variable Y, predicted by one or more independent variables (X's) in a statistical regression equation)

t = $_{df}$Student's t (an inferential statistic for testing the significance of the difference between two group means)

X = $_{df}$independent variable (often symbolizes a predictor in statistics for multiple regression analysis, or in ANOVA)

x = $_{df}$variable x, which can be assigned a numerical value; also refers to horizontal axis in Cartesian Coordinate System (from algebra and geometry)

Y = $_{df}$dependent variable (often symbolizes the predicted variable in statistics for multiple regression analysis, or in ANOVA)

y = $_{df}$variable y, which can be assigned a numerical value; also refers to vertical axis in Cartesian Coordinate System (from algebra and geometry)

Index

academic learning time (ALT) vii, xix, xxi, 63, 94–102, 119, 125
acknowledgments xix, 122
activate (for IPTAT registration) 14, 17, 22, 25, 59
activation *see* First Principles of Instruction
ALT *see* academic learning time
Analysis of Patterns in Time (APT): APT query 48, 68, 70–1, 95, 126, 128; APT temporal map v, xii, xxii, 4–6, 9–24, 44–52, 57, 63, 66, 71, 73, 84, 90, 93, 95, 99–100, 105–6, 111, 126–7; discovery of Google Analytics for doing APT vi, 46–47, 115–16; joint event occurrences vii, 63, 99–100; predictive APT query vi, 48; Nonmetric Temporal Path Analysis (NTPA) xvi, 7, 62, 76, 112, 119, 123, 127; retrodictive APT query vi, 48–49; sequential event occurrences vii, 88, 105
anonymous asynchronous online discussion 68
application *see* First Principles of Instruction
APT query *see* Analysis of Patterns in Time
APT *see* Analysis of Patterns in Time
APT temporal map *see* Analysis of Patterns in Time
asynchronous online discussion vii, 68–71
authentic problems (tasks) *see* First Principles of Instruction

big data analysis methods 108–9
big study v–vii, ix, x, xv–xvii, xx, 6, 9–27, 46–62, 71–2, 75, 93, 97, 102, 106

causal explanation 3, 74, 106, 108
certificant (passed a CT) xxi, 20–6, 42
certification tests (CT) (IPTAT) vi, ix–xvii, xxi, 9–43, 46–58, 97–100, 102, 106, 115–6, 125, 127
client ID (GA) xxi, 17, 26, 54–56
Coleman study 5–6, 117, 123
course evaluation *see* Teaching and Learning Quality (TALQ) Scales
COVID vi, 44, 116, 125
CT *see* certification tests

dabblers (IPTAT user type) vi, xviii, 40–3
demographics (registered IPTAT users) xviii, 58–61
demonstration *see* First Principles of Instruction
descriptive statistics xx, 89, 106, 127
diffusion of innovations (DOI) theory xix, 78, 82–7, 92, 125
Diffusion Simulation Game (DSG) vii, xviii–xix, 78–92, 121, 125
digraph theory 112, 119
direct instruction (DI) vii, xxii, 63–66, 78, 125, 127
discovery of Google Analytics for doing APT vi, 46–47, 115–16
DSG *see* Diffusion Simulation Game

130 Index

EDM *see* educational data mining
educational data mining 106–10, 113–14, 125–6
episodic stories (story, narrative, qualitative method) v, xviii–xix, 3–4, 31, 45, 62, 72–3, 121

First Principles of Instruction (FPI) i, v, ix–xx, 6, 7, 18–27, 29, 31, 42, 44–58, 76, 94–5, 97–103, 106, 111, 113, 115–6, 121, 126: activation v–vi, xxi, 13–23, 30–3, 51–7, 97–9, 111; application v–ix, xvii, xxi, 18–24, 30–6, 51–7, 97–9; authentic problems (tasks) vi, 18, 30–1, 78, 91, 96–9; demonstration v–ix, xvii, xxi, 13–24, 30–4, 51–7, 84, 87, 96–102, 122; integration v–vi, xvii, xxi, 13–25, 30–7, 50–3, 97–9
formative evaluation vii, xviii, 78–90
FPI *see* First Principles of Instruction

GA *see* Google Analytics
GA4 *see* Google Analytics 4
general systems theory 111, 119, 127
Google Analytics (GA) vi–vii, ix, xii, xv–xxi, 5, 7, 14, 17, 20, 22–7, 40–3, 46–59, 62–3, 71–2, 74–6, 90, 95, 97, 102, 106, 111, 115–16, 124, 126
Google Analytics 4 (GA4) vii, xvi, xx, 47–9, 56–8, 75, 126

how to recognize plagiarism *see* Indiana University Plagiarism Tutorials and Tests

Indiana University Plagiarism Tutorials and Tests (IPTAT) v–vii, xi–xxi, 6–62, 71–5, 90, 93–107, 111, 115–16, 124–6
inductive inference vii, xix, 104–6
inferential statistics 104–5, 120, 128
information theory 111, 119, 122, 127
instructional (course) evaluation i, vii–ix, xi, xv, xviii–xix, 7, 48, 75–94, 103, 110, 112, 124
instructional design (instructional development, learning design) i, v, vii, viii, xi–xvi, xviii, 18–20, 27–45, 62, 66, 71, 77–92, 109–11, 113–14
instructional effectiveness i, iii, ix, xi–xix, 4–6, 27, 29, 45–58, 74, 78, 90–1, 95, 97, 102–3, 106, 113, 115–6, 122
integration *see* First Principles of Instruction
IPTAT design and structure 18–22, 29–40
IPTAT *see* Indiana University Plagiarism Tutorials and Tests

joint event occurrences (APT) vii, 63, 99–100

LA *see* learning analytics
learning achievement 1, 5, 26, 47, 59–60, 74, 95, 100, 102–3, 109, 116–18, 124
learning analytics (LA) xii–xix, 106–14, 126–7
learning design *see* instructional design
learning journey v–ix, xi–xvi, xx, 1–9, 11–27, 42, 48–58, 63–4, 106, 112
Likert scale xix, 97–8, 125, 127–8
linear models approach (statistical) vii, xvi, xxii, 2–7, 62–4, 76, 104, 112, 118–20, 122, 124, 126

macrolevel data 107
mainstreaming (inclusion, students with disabilities) 117, 124
Map & Analyze Patterns & Structures Across Time (MAPSAT) xix, 7, 76, 111–13, 125–6
MAPSAT *see* Map & Analyze Patterns & Structures Across Time
Markov chain theory 111, 119
massive open online course *see* MOOC
mastery learning xii, xxi, 6–7, 76, 94–103
mastery tests (IPTAT) 13–16, 21, 24, 52
measure relations *see* APT and MAPSAT
mesolevel data 107
microlevel data 107
minimalists (IPTAT user type) vi, xviii, 40–3
model verification (simulation) vii, 81, 86–92
Moneyball vii, xvii, 5, 7, 63, 72–3, 77
MOO-TALQ viii, xxi, 95–102, 126
MOOC x, xii, xvi, 6, 28, 45, 62, 76, 96, 103, 124, 126
multiple regression analysis 117–19, 128
MySQL vii, xiii, 42–3, 54–9, 126

non-certificant (did not pass a CT) xxi, 20–26
Nonmetric Temporal Path Analysis (NTPA) xvi, 7, 62, 76, 112, 119, 123, 127
NTPA *see* Nonmetric Temporal Path Analysis

online teaching/learning (e-learning) i–ii, vii, ix–xix, 6–7, 9, 17, 27–62, 68–9, 71, 76–7, 82–91, 93–103, 115–16, 126
Oregon Trail metaphor (learning journey) v, xvii, 1–6, 26, 47, 104–5

PHP xiii, 12, 46, 55, 83, 85, 127
plagiarism tutorials *see* Indiana University Plagiarism Tutorials and Tests (IPTAT)
praxiological (practical) knowledge 6, 121
prediction vi, xix, 4–5, 47–8, 64–6, 72–4, 81, 87, 89, 105–9, 117, 128
predictive APT query *see* Analysis of Patterns in Time
probability theory 111, 120

qualitative knowledge 3, 105
qualitative research methods i, v, xii, xv, xvii, 3–6, 34, 63, 81–2, 104–9, 112, 119
quantitative knowledge *see* theoretical knowledge
quantitative research methods i, v, xii, xv, xvii, 2–3, 6, 63, 81, 104, 107–8, 112, 119–20

registrant (register for IPTAT) vi, xix, xxi, 27, 42, 56–9
research method xiv, xv, 2–6, 19, 63–77, 105–10, 119–20
retrodictive APT query *see* Analysis of Patterns in Time
retroductive inference 111

sabermetrics xviii, 73
sample (in statistics, representativeness of, random) 3–4, 104–6, 121
segmenting (within temporal maps, GA sessions) vi, xvii, xx, 6, 48–53, 57, 62, 71–2, 75, 111–2, 115, 128
selection bias 3–4, 104–105

sequential analysis 74, 119–20, 122
sequential event occurrences (APT) vii, 88, 105
session (Google Analytics, APT temporal map) xxii, 12–20, 40, 52, 55–58
set theory 111, 127–8
simulation (computer, games) *see* Diffusion Simulation Game
simulation fidelity vii, 79–80, 91
socioeconomic status (SES) 5, 117–18, 127
state-trait approach to measurement v, 2–5, 63, 104
student engagement xx, 64–66, 102, 118–20, 125
student learning journey *see* learning journey
successful student engagement *see* academic learning time
summative evaluation (assessments) 90, 109
system structural properties *see* Map & Analyze Patterns & Structures Across Time
system temporal properties *see* Map & Analyze Patterns & Structures Across Time

TALQ *see* Teaching and Learning Quality Scales
teacher-student interaction vii, 66
Teaching and Learning Quality (TALQ) Scales vii–viii, ix, xii–xix, 7, 76, 93–103, 126–7
temporal map v, xii, xxii, 4–6, 9–24, 44–52, 57, 63, 66, 71, 73, 84, 90, 93, 95, 99–100, 105–6, 111, 126–7 *see also* Analysis of Patterns in Time
temporal segmenting *see* segmenting; *see also* Analysis of Patterns in Time
theoretical (quantitative) knowledge 104–105, 110
theory, value of 110–11
traditionalists (IPTAT user type) vi, xviii, 40–3

UA *see* Universal Analytics
unique pageview (Google Analytics) vi, xxi, 22–25, 50–55
Universal Analytics (UA) vii, xvi, 14, 47–58, 75, 127

For Product Safety Concerns and Information please contact our EU representative GPSR@taylorandfrancis.com
Taylor & Francis Verlag GmbH, Kaufingerstraße 24, 80331 München, Germany